GROW YOUR
VALUE

GROW YOUR
VALUE

LIVING AND WORKING
TO YOUR FULL POTENTIAL

MIKA BRZEZINSKI

WEINSTEIN
BOOKS

Printed in the United States of America.

Editorial production by *Marra*thon Production Services.
www.marrathon.net

Book Design by SD Designs

Cataloging-in-Publication data for this book is available
from the Library of Congress.

ISBN: 978-1-60286-268-5 (print)
ISBN: 978-1-60286-269-2 (e-book)

Published by Weinstein Books
A member of the Perseus Books Group
www.weinsteinbooks.com

Weinstein Books are available at special discounts for bulk
purchases in the U.S. by corporations, institutions and other
organizations. For more information, please contact the
Special Markets Department at the Perseus Books Group,
2300 Chestnut Street, Suite 200, Philadelphia, PA 19103,
call (800) 810–4145, ext. 5000, or
e-mail special.markets@perseusbooks.com.

First edition

10 9 8 7 6 5 4 3 2 1

To Jim, Emilie, and Carlie

CONTENTS

Contents

WHY KNOWING YOUR VALUE ISN'T ENOUGH

"I HATE YOU, I HATE YOU, I HATE YOU!"

My daughter's words were the gutting end to a savage week. I was exhausted. My professional life starts way before the sun comes up, and it often keeps churning late into the night. Every day I fight the same endless battle that many other women do as I try to juggle my duties at work and at home. But sixteen-year-old Carlie's words struck me between the eyes. The truth was, I had failed again.

The week began as it always does with a 3:30 a.m. wakeup call. After pulling myself from bed, making the commute into Manhattan, and sitting zombie-like in a makeup chair, I read every newspaper and editorial page to prepare for *Morning Joe*, the daily morning news program that I cohost with

Joe Scarborough. Then I start planning the three-hour show in three minutes—that's all the time we generally have because my intellectually gifted and maddeningly frustrating cohost wanders into 30 Rock about exactly three minutes before we go on air. After that, Joe Scarborough and I walk to the studio, without notes, teleprompters, or safety nets. Having my job is a great honor, and I recognize that—but its pace is exhausting.

When our stage manager, Jen, gestures for the final wrap, *Morning Joe* may be over, but a long day off-camera is about to begin. On this particular Monday I was rushed off the set and into another studio to interview fashion icon and former *Vogue* editor-at-large Andre Leon Talley. Because Andre is a joyous show in himself, the interview went so far over that my producer, Rachel Campbell, had to race in to pull me off the set for my next event, which was in Philadelphia. The speech I would be giving, two hours south of Manhattan, was for our bosses at Comcast, so everyone in the office wanted me to be on time for it. A late grand entrance from my cohost Joe would be the subject of playful ribbing and laughs. But I have to play by the "good girl" rules: show up promptly, look put together, make it all seem easy.

Perhaps a normal person would have a moment for a bathroom break and to put on comfortable shoes to travel. My heels were beginning to feel like stilts, and I was desperate to pee as I ran into the auditorium with 450 elegant women waiting to hear my speech. I felt faint because I hadn't eaten all day. But all that would have to wait. The stage manager grabbed me by the arm and whispered, "You're up now. Here's the mic. Good luck!" I reached into my bulging purse, pulled out a few stray pieces of paper, and began reading off the notes I had scratched out. My assignment was to explain how women can earn their full value at work.

In my book *Knowing Your Value: Women, Money, and Getting What You're Worth* and in my Know Your Value conferences, I share stories of my own vulnerability. Whether I'm doing the show with Joe, giving a speech, moderating a panel at an event, or hosting a conference to empower women professionally, my approach is to address what *hasn't* worked for me and how I fixed it. Opening up in this way is a great start to getting to the next level. If nothing else, I'm honest, and it's my experience that people appreciate honesty.

Let's face it: our lives—as working women, as mothers, as wives—are not easy. At all. And when I am open about that and share what frankly doesn't work, at least for me, it seems to help women to see how to take that first step in knowing their own value. That is, they stop beating up on themselves for what they believe they *haven't* pulled off perfectly and begin to recognize how much work and life experience they bring to the table every day. That's what I mean by "knowing your value." It's understanding at a professional and financial level that you—your career, perspective, hard-earned lessons, and proven techniques—are greater than the sum of your parts as a working woman. You know what you're worth in the marketplace because you've earned your stripes, you know where—and how—you stand out in your field, and you know how much you should be compensated for it.

Because I've learned to appreciate my own value after many years, I don't mind telling you that the speech was a total success that day. The audience of professional women had more questions than time would allow, and I was hugged—a lot—as I raced out the door. But there was no time to enjoy the moment.

I rocketed back home—well, let's say "crawled"—in what turned out to be five hours of traffic, just in time to have missed dinner with my younger daughter, Carlie, and my husband, Jim. They are used to me being late—if I get home in time to eat with them at all. And now I had to flop into unconsciousness: the 3:30 a.m. alarm comes quickly. I took medication because I needed to sleep right away. This is often the most depressing part of my day: getting in bed alone and praying that I can get some shut-eye. Because everyone else in my life is humming along on a different clock, my schedule exacts a hefty price on my emotional well-being. A day that is so full can feel very empty and out of sync at the end. In addition to that, at some point this medication is going to catch up with me. I have to pick my poison: no sleep and the pain of exhaustion, or sleep and grow increasingly dependent on the medication. This is not really a glamorous life. This is a life of sometimes bad but always hard choices.

So that was Monday.

Tuesday was the same routine. I woke up at 3:30 a.m. and rushed to do three hours of live TV. After I stepped off the *Morning Joe* set, I ran three back-to-back sponsor meetings about Know Your Value conferences and the movement I'm building to help women know and grow their value. These are the toughest kind of meetings—those that involve getting corporations behind my message. After that, I dashed like a greyhound across town to pick up the script for a speech I was giving that night at a gala event downtown. Then I quickly got my hair done and figured out an outfit. The Wall Street fete was something I should have never agreed to. I felt exhausted and guilty on stage at Cipriani speaking to four hundred tipsy advertisers, knowing I should have been home. The event seemed like a great branding opportunity when *Adweek* invited me six months before, but now all I could do was try to figure out how to get out by 10, home by 11, and hopefully be asleep by 11:15 (if I remembered to take that medicine on my way off the stage—what is wrong with this picture?).

Wednesday: up well before the sun again to host the show, then two back-to-back meetings. After that, I flew to Washington, DC, with Joe to cover the breaking news that the director of the Secret Service had just resigned. Then I hosted a panel about a retrospective of artwork by my mother, sculptor Emilie Brzezinski, at the Phillips Collection. Afterward I raced across town to watch as my father, former National Security Advisor Zbigniew Brzezinski, had an institute named after him at the Center for Strategic and International Studies. (Attending these events made my parents happy, and I was glad I'd made the effort.)

Again, I understand that these are terrific problems for anyone to have, but truthfully? I was running on empty. Speaking of which, I drove back to New York via Baltimore; I hadn't seen my older daughter, Emilie, since I'd dropped her off at Johns Hopkins University for her freshman year earlier that fall. We had a blast! I took her on a little shopping excursion and then finally pulled in the driveway at home at about seven o'clock at night. I was trying to cram all the pieces of my life into one day by getting home at a reasonable hour, leaving me bedraggled and a bit shaky after that sixteen-hour whirlwind. But my parents were happy. Check. Emilie was happy. Check. My many brand-development efforts were humming along. Check.

However, nothing could prepare me for the next maelstrom in that grueling day: Hurricane Carlie. She's got my number, and she knows what buttons to press. Before I'd even put down my bag, Carlie sped in through the front door in her track uniform and bolted up the stairs to her room. No hug. No "Hi, Mom!" Just a glare that felt like an assault weapon with a silencer.

I stood in the front hallway, barely conscious. I took a moment to lead myself through a mental sequence. Work was finished for the day. I was at home now. It was Wednesday. I could smell dinner from the kitchen. It was time to eat. As I slowly began to shift from *"Morning Joe/*Know Your Value Mika"* to Mom, I reminded myself that research says that when kids eat dinner with their families, they do less drugs and don't get into trouble with alcohol. So I called up to her, forcefully: "Carlie, come downstairs and have dinner with us right now!" No response. I marched upstairs and had to coax her down into the kitchen. I was like that ham-fisted mom from *Modern Family*, except not as cute. And then, out of nowhere, the verbal barrage began.

"I HATE YOU! I HATE YOU! I HATE YOU!" she screamed, tears springing from her eyes. "Look at you—you're disgusting! You're a hypocrite! You're never here!" Before I could open my mouth, she sprinted back upstairs and slammed her door. What was even worse was that she had a point. I *am* rarely home for dinner during the week. And when I am home, I am always urging Jim and the girls to eat way earlier than they would like to, so I can join them and get to bed at an early hour.

I love my job. I love the work I do on behalf of empowering women. And I have to admit: I also thrive on the pace. Mostly. But some weeks are what I call "reset" weeks: the days become such a blur that I need to turn off, press the "reset" button, and gather my wits before carrying on with my crazy sprint. So this was a reset moment. Something had to give— but what? I am not sure how the schedule got so screwed up. I'm not sure who was to blame, but I sat on the stairs, still in my coat, holding all my bags, crushed. I got a lot of love at the conference in Philly, at my job, in my book signings. But that night I got none in my own home.

In fact, for women, it often seems that hard work just doesn't pay off. Although I did get to see my parents in DC and my older daughter in Baltimore, my husband and younger daughter had been put on hold. Again.

HUGGING TOTAL STRANGERS

It had been an amazing year in terms of professional value-building. Knowing one's value is huge to me. In fact, this topic plays a profound, consuming role in my life: helping women to appraise their own worth in their careers, to evaluate and appreciate the breadth of their work experience, and to feel confident asking for what they need when they enter salary negotiations.

I wrote the book *Knowing Your Value* because I'd spent decades learning how to put a qualitative and quantitative number on the experience I brought to the table. For years I'd undersold myself, apologized for asking for a raise, and meekly accepted whatever was offered. I'd bungled salary discussions with bosses by trying to imitate what I imagined a man would do—which was a disaster, let me tell you. I wanted my book to help working women learn how to assert themselves and to realize that knowing their value is tough but critical in getting their worth and being adequately compensated in the marketplace.

And to my amazement and happiness, the book had received the kind of success I had never expected. Ever since it was released in 2011, women have been coming up to me on the street, telling me that *Knowing Your Value* had given them the courage to ask for—and get—raises at their jobs. I find myself hugging total strangers to congratulate them. I feel an enormous sense of gratitude that I have played a small but important part in so many amazing women's lives. The reaction has been so strong that I decided the topic needed more attention. I started saving testimonials from women who had used the advice in my book to get a raise. That was when I began to grow the value of my own brand, and at that point, it was up to me to develop it.

Then, in the spring of 2014, I hosted my first annual Know Your Value conference in Hartford, Connecticut. There I spoke to a surprisingly jam-packed audience. I had set up the whole thing myself. I hired a team from Hartford, worked the phones to get sponsors to cover the costs of the event, and alerted the local media about it. They were happy to cover it, given the marketability of the subject matter. The event sold out; evidently there were more women hungry to hear this message than I'd even realized. This brand and its message was finding its footing! Gayle King was my keynote speaker for the day, and as she walked off stage, she pointed at me and said, "Mika, you are on to something here—Wow!"

So, along with a panel of experienced professional women, I made the point that, instead of complaining that "It's not fair!" that women get paid 77 cents to a man's dollar, we need to do what successful men have always done. We need to perform painstaking sleuthing to know our competition inside and out. It is our responsibility to compare, evaluate, and define our own experiences and set of skills. We must identify our strongest personality assets, such as being "focused," "thoughtful," and "cooperative." We should express this directly and succinctly to our higher-ups in order to get the salary and position we deserve. Because if we don't know our value and communicate it cogently, confidently, and with hard evidence, then we, as women, will never get our due. The day was full of great advice on how to do all this.

I also came up with an idea that really brought the message home—a bonus competition in which I chose five finalists based on auditions in which they pitched their value. I asked the five women to join me onstage and to deliver their two-minute pitches summing up why they deserved the $10,000 prize. And it was flat-out amazing. One woman had just undergone heart surgery forty-eight hours beforehand, yet she confidently made the case that she would use the money for a website for her small business in Madison, Connecticut. One mother of eight wanted to get her college degree to advance in her professional life and to provide for her family in the way they deserved. Another woman, soft-spoken but full of ideas and promise, broke down in tears on stage, struggling with her pitch. I held her hands. "It's hard work to state your value, but you can do it," I said. And she did. In the end every woman onstage and those I got to speak to in the audience said how much they had learned about how to put themselves out there and how to actually succeed in their careers. By the end of it I was wiping away tears myself. We had all made breakthroughs in realizing our value.

But on that Wednesday in 2014—the day when my career and my daughter's tantrum converged—I felt a distinct absence of any self-worth at all. It was as if there were two Mikas in the room. There was "Morning Mika" and "Know Your Value Mika," who could be characterized as a brand. By assertively promoting and marketing my professional brand and message, I had successfully advocated for myself, negotiated for commensurate compensation, and earned many opportunities to share what I knew with women everywhere. I was proud that I was helping so many women; it was an incredible feeling of worth and accomplishment. I actually felt that I had a calling.

But standing in the hallway in the wake of Carlie's rage, I felt empty. I certainly didn't feel that I'd arrived anywhere that could be described as "success." I felt like I do every night—exhausted, depleted. But even worse, I felt like a failure in the worst way—that I had no value at all. What was the point of all my career accomplishments if the most important people in my life felt I had pulled away from them—and if they were pulling away from me?

GROW THE DEFINITION AND REACH OF YOUR VALUE

When I was at the beginning of my career in my twenties, I thought I'd feel on top of the world once I reached the peak of my success. But somehow it just isn't like that. I can feel totally in charge at work. Even though it is stressful, my job really fits me. I love connecting with our guests. I love the energy. I absorb it, respond to it, and give it back. I'm Joe's foil as well as his wingman. I know what my value is at work. It is an incredible honor to enjoy this success, and it feels like a gift to be able to share it with others. And yes, if I can, I hope to work for a long time to come.

Then I leave work, drive home, and open the front door of my house. And the energy is different. Distant. Subtler. More primal. I have to shift gears, and my sense of my value begins to wobble. My daughters are not my young producers on *Morning Joe*. They are not constantly zipping around from the set to the green room, chattering nonstop into headsets, robo-dialing to book guests, rushing in with a late guest—nor should they be. I've never expected my daughters to be anything other than their own beautiful souls. I love them exactly the way they were when they were first born; I love them exactly the way they are now, and I always will. Period.

But still. From the constant chatter and verbal sparring with my colleagues at work, I often come home to a quiet, remote, door-closed world. I pepper my girls and husband with questions about their days, making overly chipper attempts at conversation. But I can see them cringe at all that intense energy I bring home with me. And that triggers my maternal brain to eclipse my work brain, reminding me of many of the very things my own mother told me when I first had my children: *Mika, you need to slow down. You need to be present with your family, not multitasking or taking phone calls during conversations, not vamping for the camera. Your always-on work mode isn't what your family needs, nor is it what they value in you.* So I try to transition, but it feels forced. My work has changed me . . . at least that's what it feels like they are thinking.

My mother was recently in the hospital. With the help of a little medication, she gave me the best advice she'll never remember. "You are always so happy—always so 'up,'" she scoffed. "Just stop. Give it a rest. No one is *really* like that." No one who is being her authentic self at home and at work, anyway. Instead, I'm someone who is trying to be two different people in two distinct environments—and splitting at the seams in the process.

My mother was right: I had been acting bizarrely positive. Exaggeratedly so. I had effectively put on blinders, donned my "go get 'em" game face to get everything done that I needed to accomplish. In addition to my day job, I was driven to spread the message about women's need to claim their professional due and was narrowly focused on getting everything on my to-do list checked off.

My singularity of purpose enabled me—and many other women—to extract real value from my career, titles, and compensation. But on that Wednesday I felt worthless. Here at home my market brand was not only meaningless; it was, as my daughter had clearly telegraphed through her rage, damaged. My work persona wasn't working at home. I had to grow my definition and reach not just as "Morning Mika" but also as a mother and wife—as a *person*.

When I wrote *Knowing Your Value*, my focus was on helping women get adequate remuneration in the workplace. Now I was getting a cold bucket of water over my head at home. It hit me that "value" extended to my worth as a human being, to the things that I hold dear in my inner world—my relationships to my daughters, my marriage, my extended family, and my friends. I still had plenty of work to do to grow my professional value—the experiences, know-how, and style that I bring to the table—but my sense of inner value needed work too. A lot of work.

Did I really know my value to Carlie? Did I know my role and my sense of worth at home? Could I reconnect with my family and also stay on top of my career? How could I—how can any working mom—grow in both of these areas of life? Is it possible to be clear on how we can best give of ourselves as wives, partners, and mothers without compromising our careers and our professional worth and strength? This, I realized, is why merely knowing your value as a working woman was not enough.

In order to take it to the next level and *grow* our value as people, not just as professionals, women must do some very tricky math. As more and more of us break the glass ceiling, we have to measure our professional profits against our personal losses and decide what we want our real gains to be.

THE RIGHT STUFF

I know. It's a shock. It's as though you spend years pushing yourself to climb up the steep, often trip-wired trail to the top of Mount Career. You take a breather, stretching your aching muscles and congratulating yourself on your success: Hooray, you made it! But after you've recovered from the strain of the climb, feeling strong but tired, you begin to look around you, orienting yourself in this new vista, and you begin to see that Mount Career is actually just one in a mountain range. With a summit concealed in clouds and a surface that includes both rocky outcroppings and serene meadows, there is one alp that soars above the rest: Mount the Rest of Your Life. Your first response is: "Oh. My. God." Then you think, "Do I have the right stuff to navigate this terrain? And what is the right stuff, anyway? I can't even see what the top of this thing looks like!"

This is the guidebook, right here in your hands.

We definitely need to know our value, both as professionals with demanding and interesting work *and* as women with rich, complex personal lives—and we then should grow it, maximize it in every way. And in this book I'm going to show you a variety of ways in which to do this. You're going to meet successful working women who have capitalized on their earning potential while also learning how to feel some degree of peace personally. You're also going to meet women who, like most of us, are still at the trailhead, trying to figure out which path to take. You're not going to hear any sugar-coating. Instead, you will read honest accounts of the personal fallout and regrets that women have had to face as a result of being successful in their careers. You will hear about how their sense of inner value has grown anemic over time because their professional life—indeed, their very brand as experts in their fields—needs constant tending. But you will also see how these women have learned to deal with these conflicting aspirations. And perhaps you can avoid some of our mistakes.

I'm also going to show you why people-pleasing is poison and how to just stop doing it. You'll learn how to spot the enemies inside your own head and how you can keep them at arm's length, if not defeat them. In addition, you're going to hear questions that we, as a society, are all facing but aren't talking about.

In *Knowing Your Value* I showed you how not to apologize or play the victim on the job; how to leave drama at the door, be ready to walk; and most importantly, how to communicate your professional and compensatory worth effectively.

You know your professional value. Now let's grow it, and let's also grow your inner value. Let's learn how to merge the two so we can begin to lead whole, integrated, fulfilling lives.

CHAPTER ONE

WHAT'S A WOMAN WORTH?

Career, Personal Life, and Growing Your Value

I am the Queen of the Awkward Moment—and I love it. It's a trait that I've developed ever since I was a young girl moderating political debates around the dinner table, with my brothers, mother, and White House statesman father. In interviews, discussions, and meetings, I've always found that the Awkward Moment tells me almost everything I need to know about any given topic.

When I'm in the interviewer's seat, I'll lead with a few softball questions and genial banter, and then I'll throw a wrench in the works. If the others jump in right away with rapid-fire responses, either in conflict or agreement, you're definitely in for a great discussion—but you're not going to get to that brutally honest place where time stands still, the domain of discomfort and naked insecurity. No, the Awkward

Moment is a different beast altogether. It's that uneasy lull that follows a question that's so controversial, so sensitive that no one dares take it on. When it surfaces, I know that I have suddenly pinpointed a hot-button issue. I'm onto something big.

The Most Awkward Moment of my career came in the summer of 2014 when I was moderating a panel for the White House Summit on Working Families. The subject was very close to my heart: the fact that women, wives, and mothers need to learn how to understand and leverage their value in the marketplace. I was sharing the stage with some of the country's most powerful and internationally known women. Luminaries such as feminist movement leader Gloria Steinem. Political pioneers like former Speaker of the House Nancy Pelosi. Media moguls like Black Entertainment Television (BET) CEO Debra Lee. Intellectual institutional powerhouses like Judith Rodin, the former president of University of Pennsylvania and current president of the Rockefeller Foundation.

I was nervous to be up there with such incredibly accomplished women. But I was very excited to get an inside look at how they had estimated their financial value at different points in their careers—or, unless they'd been born superwomen, how they'd underestimated it. I wanted them to share what had happened in their work lives, what they'd learned, and how they'd used their experiences to maximize their monetary worth in order to accomplish such extraordinary achievements.

But I also wanted to know something else.

To be honest, I wanted to come away with some tips that I could use in my own life. Obviously, the women on this panel had done it all—at least over time, right? But how had they done it? I wanted to know all the mechanisms they'd deployed on their way up. I'm no Judith Rodin or Gloria Steinem, but I do know that more than half the time, between my job, my kids, my marriage—everything—I'm flat-out exhausted. And it doesn't feel like it's working. The scramble to take control of the important parts of my life (never mind doing the basics, such as going to the dentist) is relentless. I'm always putting out fires. I'm always on edge. And although I wouldn't trade my career for anything, there's no question that it has taken its toll on my family. So I wanted to know: What kinds of tolls had their careers taken on them? And how did they solve those problems? Getting answers to these questions would be the greatest gift of all because, as far as I'm concerned, what is the meaning of what I'm doing in my professional life if my family is not thriving?

So on that blazingly hot summer day, in a football stadium–sized conference room packed to the rafters, I began by introducing the distinguished panel. Then I asked, "What do you see out there in the ranks . . . do women always know their value? Do they communicate it effectively for themselves?" I asked whether they had observed what I have: that women are often their own worst enemies in the workplace. I had seen time and again that we don't ask for what we're worth because we don't know or we're too scared to find out what our value is.

Men aren't too scared to ask. And it's not that men get paid more than women only because they feel that they are more entitled to a bigger salary. Instead, it seems that we women don't claim our value because we don't feel entitled to it. We ask for less than what we're worth when we're applying for or offered a job or a raise. Not only that, we often apologize for what we assume is the "inconvenience" we're putting our higher-ups through when we do ask. Okay—now discuss, panel!

Right off the bat, Rockefeller Foundation President Judith Rodin confessed what happened when she was first offered the job as head of University of Pennsylvania years before. "When I was offered the presidency of Penn, the first woman Ivy League president, I think the board believed that I would— and should—feel extremely grateful." She laughed. "They offered me a salary, and I went home overnight and started to get really angry. I went back to the board the next day and I said, 'Would you have offered me that if I were a man?' And to their credit, they paused to think about it, and then within the next ten minutes they raised my salary significantly."

If that isn't an example of knowing your value, I don't know what is. Rodin's experience illustrates how critical it is for women to advocate for themselves. To know what men are getting paid for the same jobs. To know that if you're being offered the job, your employers probably have a higher estimation of your value than you do. So you've got to step it up, do your homework, and explain plainly and firmly what you bring to the table. That's the essence of knowing your professional value.

But, I said to the conference audience, it takes a while to learn how to do that. BET's Debra Lee agreed. She marveled at how different things were now from when she was rising up in the ranks as a media executive. "I'm seeing a growing trend of young women being better prepared, and saying, 'I'm not going accept a position, if I'm not [compensated fairly].'" She added, "When I was coming along, I didn't have that many role models, in terms of women and business or female CEOs. I never even thought about being a CEO." When she was first offered the position of chief operating officer (COO) at BET, she'd learned that three men at the company had already applied for it. But there had been no job posting! How in the world did these men have the wherewithal, the guts, to apply for a position that didn't even exist?

"They just make stuff up! They oversell in every way!" Debra said.

I couldn't resist breaking in, throwing my hands up in disgust and admiration. "It is an unbelievable talent on the part of the human male!" We all, audience included, had to laugh. Evidently just about everyone in the room had had a run-in with that "unbelievable talent on the part of the human male" at one time or another. Debra confessed that even when she had been invited to make stuff up—stuff like her salary, for example—she had so little sense of her professional value—her skills, her experience, her unique perspective, her earned wisdom and judgment—that she couldn't even imagine what the number attached to it might even look like. When she'd been taken out for lunch and was offered the COO position and was then asked how much she wanted,

Debra admitted that she was astounded. "I was like, 'Wow—I can pick a number?'" she recalled thinking at the time, chuckling at her naïveté. "I hadn't thought about that. So I said, 'Well . . . I don't know. A million dollars sounds good.' And he looked at me. And he said, 'Why so low?'"

On the surface of it, the panel was going great. The speakers were sharing stories of how they'd learned to measure what they were worth professionally and financially in a take-it-to-the-bank kind of way. The audience was getting a lot of information about how these pros had paved the roads to their brilliant careers. But still, women in the audience and online weren't getting exactly what they wanted to hear. And neither was I. In the moderator's seat I was being handed stacks of questions from these women. Perhaps not coincidentally, most of them centered on the very theme I was dying to hear these women talk about: How had they managed to do it all on their way up—and what were the consequences in their personal lives? I could feel the Awkward Moment approaching.

"So I'm getting a lot of questions," I said nervously, flipping through the stack. "I'm going to encapsulate, because they reflect something I wanted to know too." I hesitated, wondering how I was going to frame this discussion. But even as Queen of the Awkward Moment, asking these women about how their personal lives had collided with their careers was going to be, well, difficult. This question was so intimate that for the first time in a long time, I found myself stalling. "The women who are sending in questions are starting out or halfway there in their careers, and you all are at the top," I stammered. "You have dynamic careers . . ." I paused—why were my palms sweating? Finally I asked, in the gentlest possible way, "Any unexpected personal strain from that?"

Silence. Replaced momentarily by forced laughter. Followed by more silence. Oh, God. I looked around at each panelist to see who was going to take this question on. Nothing. Nancy Pelosi looked as if she smelled something bad. Some audience members did too. "Well," Debra Lee finally said, stiffly, "maybe none that I want to talk about." And clammed up. No one else was biting. I knew it would be a touchy subject, but this was like yanking out wisdom teeth without anesthesia. It was remarkable to consider that these women had chatted about their strategies for increasing their earnings and power as if they'd been swapping vacation stories. But on the subject of how their careers' successes had impacted their personal lives? Nada. At least there had been one response, so I had something to go on with Debra. I could pull this one out, get us out of this pit of weird discomfort. I had to. The Awkward Moment is only valuable to the extent that it's followed by a watershed moment in which a surprising and raw truth is revealed. So I persisted.

"Debra, you talked about your life changing and you not even imagining being CEO. So how did you know what that would feel like personally?" I asked. "Do you feel like you have to 'edit' around the people around you? Do you feel like you can be who you are at work, at home?" Again, nothing. The panelists shifted in their chairs—some blankly gazed out at the crowd, some smiled politely at me. But they simply would not talk.

This was fast becoming not just an Awkward Moment, but an aggravating one too. I'll admit it: I was annoyed. I couldn't believe these smart, gritty professional women would share with complete candor about the discriminatory struggles they'd had in their careers but remain lips-sewn on how their work lives had affected their marriages, partnerships, friendships, family, and children. These were real and important experiences for all working women, mothers, and wives to learn and share about, but the women who were supposed to be role models were refusing to go there. I grew even more insistent. "I mean, these are questions, I think, that we should put on the table—should we not?" I asked. "Or are we all going to say, 'It's so easy. We're awesome. All of our relationships are perfect. And you can do it too!'"

And . . . silence. Not the kind of silence that people are compelled to fill with embarrassed coughing or throat-clearing. A complete sound blackout. Crickets chirping. After what seemed like a purgatorial eternity, former Speaker Nancy Pelosi jumped in and changed the subject entirely. I shifted gears, and the show went on.

But I couldn't stop thinking about what had happened.

If their work and personal lives were beautifully intertwined, they would have happily shared it. Instead, they'd been mute. The takeaway for me was that successful women evidently felt too insecure and vulnerable to talk about how work had influenced their relationships and their sense of worth in their whole lives. In the end they were not prepared to go on the record about it.

But in this book we do. Dr. Judith Rodin and Senator Claire McCaskill will talk about how a burgeoning career can cause stress in relationships and even harm marriages—their marriages. You'll hear from PepsiCo CEO Indra Nooyi, who says she "leaves her crown at the door" every day. How tossing out her CEO persona at the threshold and playing the role of an acquiescent wife and mother is how her marriage has survived the intense demands of her career. Wow. Their honesty gave me the guts to say that I am struggling too.

PROFOUND PERSONAL CONSEQUENCES

What is success, really? Is it making a lot of money? Being at the top of your field? Fulfilled in your career? What are we chasing? And what about your personal life—doesn't "success" have a role there too? What are the deeper undertones in the meaning of "value"? We should certainly calculate our profits in terms of work experience, expertise, and money. But what about outside the workplace? What's the calculus for that? And how does our inner sense of purpose compare, qualitatively, to the value in our careers? Are they oceans apart or next-door neighbors? Can they complement each other? Or at least coexist without our having a nervous breakdown or massive identity crisis?

These questions—and so many successful women's reluctance to go near them—haunt, baffle, and, often, just plain elude me. I've speculated that one of the reasons these women skate over their personal lives or simply refuse to talk about them altogether is because women are still unrepresented at the highest levels of power: corporate, political, academic, scientific, and more.

For example, less than 5 percent of the top companies have women as CEOs. Slightly more than 10 percent of the 1,645 "Forbes' World's Billionaires of 2014" are women. As of this writing, there are only fourteen incumbent female heads of state. Perhaps their lips are sealed about their wrenching inner conflicts because no established woman would ever want to say anything to discourage younger women from aiming higher than the glass ceiling. One of the most powerful CEOs in the world told me that men are always bringing their wives to family retreats, yet women managers never bring their husbands. *Never.* Think about that. What is that telling your boss? What are we hiding? Why do we feel that we have to keep our personal lives and professional lives separate, even when we're invited to merge them for a day or two? Is it because we, as women, don't want to be seen as "wives" in a workplace setting? Are we worried that the presence of our husbands would somehow compromise our authority in the eyes of our colleagues?

We know that many Millennial women are burning out before they turn thirty. So the question must be asked: If the life of a highly successful, working woman is so complicated, why would anyone want it—much less to be a full-stop, executive, all-consuming "success"? And yet is it right for women who have been handsomely rewarded for their relentless work ethic to claim that there haven't been profound personal consequences in other areas of their lives? As I blurted out at the White House panel, "Are we all going to say, 'It's so easy! We're awesome! All of our relationships are perfect! And you can do it, too!' "? Come on, now. If that were true, there would be many more of us making it to the top.

I think we all know firsthand—or, if you're young, you've at least suspected—that such toss-offs are flat-out frauds. In my life, the reality on the ground is that it has never, ever been easy. It has not always been awesome. And my relationships—perfect? Where do I even start?

My daughters have grown up often feeling annoyed because I am not like my friend Beth. Beth is an awesome stay-at-home mother of twin girls in my town. She was always able to have Halloween parties and show up at all school events. As our daughters got older and all became runners on the high school track team, Beth was the leader of the "parent pack." I never knew where to go during cross-country meets. No worries: Beth had mapped it out. All I had to do was follow Beth and her camera (yes, she took all the pictures at every school event). My older daughter, Emilie, once asked me, "Why can't you be like *her*?"

It's true: I've missed school plays, birthday parties, sporting events, back-to-school nights—you name it. You can't be in two places at once, so you have to do the math. I often made decisions with the big picture in mind. It has paid off in terms of my career, but not without many moments when my heart hurt. There have been genuine consequences, some so distressing that I don't want to go any further because it would compromise my family's privacy. Suffice it to say, it has been crushing on more than a handful of occasions.

As for my husband, I suspect that he is fed up with the demands of my career. It used to be funny when friends and colleagues would laughingly call Jim, whose last name is Hoffer, "Mr. Brzezinski." It isn't funny anymore. Jim would tell you that he spends too many nights eating dinner alone while I am still in Manhattan at some gala or work-related event, surrounded by a gaggle of strangers whom I will never see again. I regret every second I am away from my family at night, but I feel I am required to be at these functions. At first, going to such glam affairs was exciting, I guess, but after a while it all blurs. I feel awful about missing family time, and I often overcompensate when I'm home by lavishing too much attention on my family, buying them things, or trying to stuff ten conversations into one.

But at the same time, if you want to be at the top of your game, long hours are nonnegotiable. Just ask Indra Nooyi, who worked eighteen-hour days when her children were small. Being successful isn't just a question of doing a killer job during business hours. You'd better be out there networking on behalf of your organization—and yourself. You'd better be mentally, physically, and sartorially "on" for professional events. You'd better be ready to travel—maybe a lot. And for some reason, we feel like we have to fill the same amount of space at home. Later you'll hear from my friend Senator Claire McCaskill about how she would finish a case as a prosecutor—putting away a man for life—and then rush home to frantically make dinner from scratch. Talk about an exhausting double life.

I'm not saying that women whose partners' jobs regularly involve travel don't feel the unnatural silence that settles on their homes, don't feel abandoned at times because it feels as if their husbands prioritize work over family. But when it's a woman walking in those career shoes—a wife, a mother—the fallout is far, far different, and the fallout begins with how you feel about yourself.

For one thing, as a society, we're still not used to successful working women—not by a long shot. There have been many changes, for sure, and one of the most interesting to me is that the number of powerhouse women in finance with stay-at-home spouses has climbed nearly tenfold since 1980. The Mrs. Executive Homemakers, Wives-in-Chief, and all those Mrs. Robinsons—women who historically hosted fancy networking dinners and organized the executive male golf outings, all to support their Wall Street husbands' careers—might be fading from view. But still, there's no question that in our culture, we're more comfortable with the idea of men making the lion's share of household income.

According to our exclusive MSNBC Working Women Study Poll conducted for this book, male breadwinners are more likely to have always held this traditional role in the relationship. To be specific, eight in ten (84 percent) male breadwinners have always been the primary earner, compared with just six in ten (58 percent) female breadwinners. And I still detect a whiff of suspicion, even of disapproval, toward working women, specifically mothers. Although I am capable of feeling guilty and paranoid where my working-mom status is concerned, according to statistics, I'm decidedly not. Americans are still remarkably entrenched in Eisenhower-era thinking when it comes to their attitudes toward working mothers.

More than 70 percent of mothers in the United States work outside the home. Yet according to a 2013 Pew study, only 16 percent of American adults say that the best growing environment for a young child is to have a mother who works full-time. Forty-two percent believe that it's best for mothers only to work part-time. And fully one-third of Americans declare that mothers should not work outside the home at all if they want what's best for their children.

So we're not imagining it when we're in the presence of those who seem judgmental about our work and family lives, who seem to believe that we should insist, misty-eyed, that if we could, we'd quit our jobs to be stay-at-home moms. And indeed, studies have shown that a majority of American working mothers are on record as saying that they would drop out of the workplace to stay at home with the kids if they could afford to do so. But is it possible that this is merely a failure to communicate?

Because that same 2013 Pew study found that women's feelings about working outside the home have changed markedly in recent years. Among mothers with children under age eighteen, the percentage saying they would *prefer* to work full-time has increased from 20 percent in 2007 to 32 percent in 2012. Moreover, according to our MSNBC poll, breadwinner moms are more likely than female breadwinners without children to say they enjoy making most of the family money (41 percent moms, versus 32 percent non-moms).

My reading of the statistics convinces me that because many mothers have to work—and a growing number actively *want* to work—we have to openly address these hard questions about the enemies to working women's success. Women want to succeed at work, and most must work, yet we're getting the message that our career aspirations are not acceptable, that we're actively damaging our children, our families. That's an extremely worrisome message.

And really, who can't help internalizing it? If we even begin to start trying to live an integrated life, one in which we feel at peace with our professional and inner values, we can't help but feel shame and guilt. We have to talk about the fact that our sense of worth in the workplace is often worlds apart from what we mean to our families and close friends. We have to discuss how to grow our value in all areas of our lives so we can truly claim to be—and actually be—*successful*.

The problem is that no one is talking about those issues. Yet.

NOTHING SHORT OF STAGGERING

Before we get into the business of women, value, and the price of success, I'd like to pause briefly to reflect on how far women have come in terms of education and career parity in a relatively short period of time. Obviously we all know that women are catching up with men in the workplace—at mach five. But it makes sense to start the discussion of growing our value with how the United States came to recognize that women had *any* value outside the home to begin with. Because let's face it: women's growing labor parity with men—and all of the economic, sociological, and other forecasts say that young women coming up through the ranks now will supersede their male counterparts—is profoundly changing our social history.

So let's just take a minute and really think about this. Only about fifty years ago, in 1960, if you used the phrase "female breadwinner," people wouldn't have had the slightest idea of what you were talking about (or they might have suspected that you were an anarchist). Back then only 11 percent of mothers were the primary family earners. And probably most of this 11 percent were those social taboos—single mothers. But by the 1970s, thanks in large part to women flooding into colleges and the Women's Movement, females entered the labor force in droves. In the 1980s, because of ever-increasing women's education—not to mention the spiking divorce rates, which left nearly half of America's children being raised by single mothers—women flooded the workplace in far greater numbers than the decade before. (Anyone who remembers *Working Girl* starring Melanie Griffith can easily visualize that piece of women's history—Reeboks, power suits, and all.)

To wrap your mind around the leap we're talking about, consider for a moment the following US Census data. From 1940 to 1969 the number of female managers at work went up from 11 to 16 percent. Fine: that was then. But from 1970 to 1989 the percentage of female managers skyrocketed from 17 percent to nearly 40. And from then on, women's steady climb up has been nothing short of staggering (although, as mentioned, there are still comparatively few women at the helm of the state or big business).

Let's do a snapshot of the state of educational status between the sexes. In 1991, after fifty years of profound inequity, parity between young women and men in their twenties who had earned a college degree (or more) converged at about 23 percent. Less than twenty years later, young women outpaced their male counterparts in higher education, representing about 37 percent to guys' 27. And this trend is projected to soar.

While we're at it, let's get back to working mothers. That 11 percent of mom breadwinners in 1960? Today more than 40 percent of all US households with children under the age of eighteen are supported solely or primarily by mothers. Several years ago scads of shrill, anxious reports came out about women dropping out of the workforce altogether to raise their young children. But guess what? The current US Department of Labor data says that just ain't so. On the contrary, by far most mothers work for or work to contribute to a living. Seventy percent of mothers with children under eighteen work. Moms with infants? Fifty-seven percent of them work. Moms with kids under three years old? Sixty percent of them work. Sixty-four percent of moms with three- to six-year-olds are bringing home the bacon (and the paper towels, tonight's dinner, and probably a whole lot more).

And in terms of knowing our value as women in the workplace? Ladies, if I wore a hat, I would definitely take it off to you. Nearly every week or so there's new data on how women are starting to outearn men. This one, in particular, was mind-boggling to me: the total family income among married couples with kids is highest when the mother is the breadwinner, not the father. Go, Mom! And Millennial women? In regard to knowing—and getting—your value in the workplace, you are flat-out rocking it. Even though women as a group still make only 77 cents to men's dollar, women in their twenties without kids at home earn a reported $1.08 to the dollar more than men, by some estimates.

As far as the workplace goes, women have definitely arrived, or at least we're on the way up. We have stretched ourselves to take titanic strides, whether we wanted to initially or not. We have achieved astonishing successes. Hopefully you know your value as a career woman and are getting paid what you're actually worth—or at least, you're well on your way.

And so here we are, competent and, increasingly, compensated. We are getting there, at least in the numbers.

So . . . anyone know what happens next?

WHO'S GOING TO TAKE CARE OF THAT?

Working women are feeling, shall we say, highly conflicted, especially if they're breadwinners. According to our poll, female breadwinners generally have mixed feelings about being the primary earner and are less likely than male breadwinners to enjoy that role. The poll also disclosed that female breadwinners are less likely than male breadwinners to feel "proud," "content," "emotionally secure," "financially secure," and "relieved" about being the primary earner in their relationship.

Well, that's a shocker. So I am not as alone as I thought. These numbers opened my eyes. You feel that way too, don't you? And why wouldn't you? Because of today's more egalitarian partnerships and marriages, you probably assumed that you and your life partner would share managing your home and family life. The children's needs, from the logistical and physical to the emotional and intellectual. The cooking. The laundry. The housecleaning, bill-paying, repairing damaged parts of your home (or arranging for them to be repaired: "I called the plumber, and he's coming tomorrow"), and everything in between. Moreover, because you assumed that you would be dividing up these jobs, you had probably also assumed that this partnership would allow you both to flourish in your careers and to enjoy the comforts of an efficient, harmonious home. That is, you never imagined that you'd be more or less expected to handle all these things alone. Because—no offense, guys—studies show that even though married dads are helping much more with household chores than ever before, working moms still do the bulk of it.

Yes, we're cooking, cleaning, caring for children—*even if we are earning more than the men*. Even in this relatively post-sexist age, you'd be hard-pressed to find the successful, working mother who wasn't resentful that her spouse gets an all-but-free ride when it comes to family and household duties . . . unless, of course, we're talking about one of those stay-at-home-dads (SAHDs) so popular in the media these days. But I think that *we* are the problem. We *think* that we should to do it all—and if not, we are failing.

Speaking of which, can we look at this phenomenon a little more closely for a moment? The number of men who stay at home with the kids is actually slightly less than it was in the late 1990s. So why didn't the zeitgeist get much—if not more—play then? Why is it that we're hearing and reading so much about these all-business alpha women and emasculated beta men now? Hypothesis: back in the nineties women were not taking over in the workplace—thereby assuming traditionally male roles—in the record numbers that they are today. Viewed through more than one lens, whether they actively want to or not, women are toppling our normative ideal of breadwinners, heads of household, families, and husbands. Men, it has been noted in more than one media report, are getting left out, they don't know where they belong anymore, and more than a few are resentful as hell. And speaking of husbands, it seems as if the trouble really starts when she makes more than he does. Even the most gender-enlightened couples wrestle with the power dynamic triggered by a fatter paycheck for the wife—and that tension can play out in the quality of their communication, love life—even both of their senses of identity.

I'll state the obvious: success for women has a much higher price than it does for men.

Even if our work invigorates us, most of us are still stressed out. As mothers, we are exhausted and wracked with guilt when we come home at night to the angry and distant children. Or are they truly angry? Is it our own guilt, our own feeling of not doing enough that they are playing off of? Are they really distant, or are we feeling a little left out, wishing someone actually missed us? My point is: Who is getting the short end of the stick? Maybe it's not the kids.

And then there's the business of running a household. What about managing its relentlessly expanding, morphing needs? Who's going to take care of that?

And speaking of earning, who's going to manage our family budget, finances, and investments—who, exactly, is going to make the important decisions about them?

To put it in even starker terms: Who is going to take care of, to nurture this home, and who is going to feel valued in it? What does it mean when the person at the helm isn't sure of her place there? What impact does that have on the harmony of the household? I know that in my own home I walked on eggshells, overcompensated for not being around, and then paid the price because I was going through the motions of what I thought I should be doing. In some ways I wish I had settled for less but better in terms of connecting with my family. Instead of trying to cram in "being a mom" and doing "mom" activities with my kids (running the school fundraiser, being the classroom parent representative, hosting scads of sleepovers), I would have been better off putting on sweats, ordering pizza, and watching *Modern Family* with them like my husband did.

Finally—and this shouldn't come last because it's certainly not least—what about your relationship? Where's the time for your partner and you to unwind and genuinely connect with each other? In my case, if my husband and I can wolf

down a quick bite at the end of the day in each other's presence, exchanging monosyllabic code words, we basically consider that "connecting." He's in the television news business
too, and we learned a long time ago that it stops for no one.
But is there a stop sign anywhere in this landscape? Relationships may survive this, but I can't believe that they will thrive.
And, as you will read in this book, some don't survive. Many
don't. We need to talk about this.

I BARELY HAVE TIME TO GO TO THE BATHROOM

You know that your effort at work-life balance really isn't
working out very well when you find yourself pulling out
one of your temporary crowns in front of hundreds of people
because you hadn't had a second to go to the dentist. It's a
gesture that just doesn't illustrate "having it all."

My adventure in public tooth-pulling began when Arianna Huffington—astonishing businesswoman, journalist,
thought leader, and friend—invited me to cohost a conference based on her book *Thrive: The Third Metric to Redefining
Success and Creating a Life of Well-Being, Wisdom, and Wonder.*
Essentially written as a mission to help extremely successful
people achieve a work–personal life balance, the book
exhorted power brokers to move beyond goals of money and
influence and to take time instead to focus on a sense of inner
peace. I was flattered to be asked, especially as the struggle to
balance work and life describes my world and personality. I
was ripe for this assignment! I had a lot to say about it, and I

did say a lot about it. Only it wasn't exactly what was on the conference program.

This is how the promo copy on the *Thrive* website billed the conference: "Hosted by Arianna Huffington and Mika Brzezinski, *Thrive: A Third Metric Live Event*, brings together leaders from a variety of fields, including Tory Burch, Katie Couric, and Julianne Moore, to join them for a conversation about their own experiences and steps they've taken to live a more sustainable, fuller and more impactful life." Speaking to an audience of big names, executives, and other intelligentsia, Arianna and I would be hosts who were, she had written, "evangelist[s] for the need to disconnect from our always-connected lives and reconnect with ourselves." We would share our own experiences. We would talk with an impressive circle of speakers about a new way of working and thinking that could help financially flourishing people soulfully thrive—which, as Arianna described it, is the willingness to "make room for well-being, wisdom, wonder and giving." Right. Just set me in front of a teleprompter, and I was ready to go.

I had been up since 3:30 a.m., hosted *Morning Joe* from 6 to 9 a.m., and then raced to the City Center to get on stage for Thrive. I was exhausted, but reading a prompter is second nature for me, and we had spent a month planning every aspect of this event. So up came the lights, and Arianna and I stepped out on stage. Surprise! The teleprompter did not have the correct script. And what's worse, I was then told via head-set that it couldn't be fixed until the conference was all but over. So I had only one option, and that was winging it—all day long. "Thrive" had just turned into a live, extended, onstage version of *Morning Joe.*

For eight hours I improvised, but with no script to follow, I felt weird. If I had been fed the lines by the prompter, I would have been able to slip into a role of a "successful" but "mindful" person, espousing the imperative to cultivate self-care and inner knowledge. But sans script, I didn't feel like that person. I felt naked! Revealed! I felt like myself. And honestly, among all these distinguished women and meditation gurus, I felt like a complete fraud. I began to panic inside. I started to sweat. There were more than two thousand people staring at me, expecting something. I was going to have to dig deep.

I just couldn't relate without being honest about the fact that I was not thriving. Speakers were exhorting the audience to thrive by appreciating that "the only time you have to be alive is now," "it's time for you to stand up and sing your song," and that you should "give yourself permission to step into your gifts and share them with others." Because we were ad-libbing, I went with the truth. "Arianna is thriving; I am a work in progress."

Most days I barely have time to go to the bathroom. On occasion I haven't even had enough time for that. At Thrive I figured I'd keep that to myself but share my dental disaster. My life was always so relentlessly overwhelmed with work and family responsibilities that I couldn't even make it to a dental appointment. In fact, I'd been putting it off for so long that, on stage, I could feel, in my mouth, one of my crowns wiggling perilously out of its socket. It had come out a few times, and I set it back with my tongue to keep it there until I had time to go to the dentist.

And then, just like that, it actually popped out. Into my mouth. While I was trying to shove it back in with my tongue discreetly, I had a thought: What if I were to say out loud, to the audience of a couple of thousand people, that not only did I not have time to stop and wonder and be wise, but I couldn't even get a broken crown replaced? So I did say it. And I pulled out my tooth to demonstrate that I was not thriving. There was a hush and some incredulous laughter.

I told them that Arianna was my inspiration, the true symbol of the Thrive movement. But I was not quite there. Together we made for a great event. Arianna was aspirational. I was definitely relatable—with a slightly comedic edge.

PEOPLE-PLEASING IS POISON

Really—just stop it. People-pleasing? Trying to make everyone at home and at work happy all the time, killing yourself so that you never have to say "no" for fear of letting down your boss, your children, your spouse? It's poison. My mother told me the same thing that day in the hospital in her own special way. "You are just annoying. Stop it." Again, the best advice she ever gave me. I find this especially difficult to do because it is a quality that is great for your very first or second job. But I find when I am overscheduled and questioning my own worth as a professional—or as a wife and mother—I scramble around, trying to please everyone without taking care of myself. It is extremely destructive and pleases no one, least of all me.

People-pleasing will eat you alive. So stop it. Trying to pull off some Zen work-life equilibrium is like getting sucked in by a pharmaceutical ad that shows a woman so joyful and relaxed that we don't really pay attention to the underlying voiceover reading off all the pill's hair-raising side effects.

I did learn a great deal at Thrive. Arianna challenged me to redefine success. The definition of "success" is highly subjective. It means a zillion different things to a zillion different people: money, power, status—you name it. But probably you will ultimately reach a point in your life as a successful working woman, hopefully sooner than later, when you will realize that earning real success—success that will truly make you happy—is an outside *and* an inside job. You need to grow your value in your career as well as the one in your heart. That is why this book turned out to be about so much more than money. "Value" needs to be redefined and explored as we learn to develop our professional worth and rise to the top.

PROFESSIONAL VALUES VERSUS INNER VALUES

Women are pretty much doing everything, trying to be all things to all people. If that's actually working in any household, my guess is that it's doing so by the skin of its teeth. But in the advertising and marketing business such a scenario would be the kiss of death. Advertisers and marketers know that a brand that tries to be all things to all people falls flat on its face. It has no goal, no message. It doesn't know what it is—and because of that, no one else does either. How can a product that has no specific message, style, mission, and target audience ever succeed? The answer is that it can't. That's why new businesses often start out by developing the precise core and nuances of their flagship brand before they do anything else—and why the fiscal health of established businesses often depends on launching an overhaul of their brand's value to sharpen, freshen, and continue to sell.

As women, we need to do the same thing.

It might sound calculating, callous, even Machiavellian, but no matter where you are along your career path, it is absolutely essential that you know your "professional brand." You might not like to think of yourself as a can of Pepsi, but let me tell you: knowing your message is one of your most powerful assets in the marketplace. Consider the cola brand "Pepsi Max," for example. Its actual ingredients are nothing more than carbonated water, caramel coloring, the artificial sweetener aspartame, and a handful of other chemicals and natural ingredients. But no one's buying Pepsi Max for its ingredients. They're buying it for its brand value.

The message of Pepsi Max's ads is clear: guys are cool and tough enough to deal with anything—including Pepsi Max. It's a message that we end up unconsciously internalizing because we're drinking it through the media well water. There is a dedicated, brilliant ad and marketing team behind Pepsi Max, constantly creating, testing, and launching the most effective, clever, and clear ways to communicate the product's brand value. Its website, commercials, Facebook page, social media platforms, and a commercial relationship with rapper Snoop Dogg are all extensions of that brand value.

In one ad, for example, guys are placed in a variety of perilous and excruciating scenarios, and after each montage shot, the "maimed" actor says: "I'm good!" In another commercial guys call out so-called ingredients that make Pepsi Max manly and dangerously cool: scorpion venom, mace, pulverized Viking bones, rabid wolverine spit. Another has Snoop Dogg magically showing up at the supermarket to sex up Pepsi Max and make the competing diet cola look fuddy-duddy. All these campaigns comprise the scaffolding that supports the heart of Pepsi Max's brand value. But that brand value is encapsulated with the catchy, straightforward catchphrase: "Maximum Taste, No Sugar, and Maybe Scorpion Venom. Pepsi Max, the First Diet Cola for Men."

If you want to carve out a successful route for yourself in any career, you've got to do what Pepsi Max does. You've got to do what any good brand advertising or marketing executive does. Obviously you're not launching ad campaigns to showcase and extend your brand value. Your equivalent of a commercial is bringing your professional expertise, point of view, and worth ethic to the job. Just like each of the Pepsi Max ads that show different marketable attributes of the cola in various appealing ways, you harness your own expertise and style to show your boss and colleagues what you can do by working your butt off.

Focus on improving what you're doing now and not on some complex project you're planning for the future. Know the right time to present well-thought-out and professional proposals for changing what systematically hasn't been working. Describe new ways for the organization to better hone or extend its reach. Even wearing the right wardrobe can convey your brand's message. You get the idea. Essentially your efforts at work and the extent to which they are favorably noticed and appreciated are like Pepsi Max commercials. Moreover, just as all those ads support a single slogan that captures the cola's brand value, you need your own slogan of sorts that communicates your professional value.

To develop your own professional value—your brand— you must create a pithy, cogent compendium of those particular adjectives and expertise that describe what you bring to the table as a member of a work team (or as a freelance contractor, as the case may be). It might take you months or even years to gather enough experience to nail it down, but ultimately you must be able to encapsulate your professional value in a few short sentences. It's got to be as powerful as the pitch you'd deliver to the top honcho at your organization if you had the chance to bend her ear in the elevator for a few seconds. With your "ads" and pitch together, your professional value will be able to do for you what it's designed to do: get you noticed, differentiate you from the pack, and communicate quickly and articulately what you bring to the table—so that you become known as the right person for the right job.

But it is simply not enough to know your core, professional message. As women, we need to grow our value in all aspects of our lives to be nourished, energized, and successful—not simply in material ways but also in authentic joy and gratitude. To be a truly successful working woman—with or without kids, in or out of a committed relationship—you need to know your inner value. The value of your relationships, of communication and harmony in your marriage, of your home life, of your spirit, of yourself as a human being.

You need to stop simply reacting to work, to your husband or boyfriend's mood, to your desperate need for a new handbag. You've got to ask yourself hard questions about what you really want in life. You will need to have hard talks with the people you love about what they want from you—and from their own lives in general. You have to learn who you really are—your very core sense of self, which extends far beyond your professional worth.

To accomplish this, above all else, you must be absolutely honest. Don't just parrot the values you think your parents, social circle, workplace, or society wants or expects of you. Don't allow yourself to cop out and turn out a boilerplate answer: "My inner value is being an attentive, loving wife, always there for my children, and taking my career as far as it can go." That's overgeneralizing. It could very well be overreaching. And it might not describe you—or your goals and dreams—at all. If you are not specific, if you do not authentically connect to what you believe to be your inner value, you will never understand the contours of your mind, heart, and spirit. You will probably not be happy. You will definitely not be successful in the most complete sense of the term.

I realize that this is a tall order. I mean, after all, I'm telling you to take an enormous chunk of your time—and a major magnitude of mindshare—to determine your value from the outside in. Who has the time? Most of us, I'd hazard a guess, are barely keeping it together now!

And that is precisely my point. It isn't enough to barely keep things together as they are—not for you, and not for me. It is precisely because I pulled my cracked tooth out of my mouth and held it up in front of a live audience and am always frenetically trying to connect with my husband and family, that I have had to assess my professional value as well as my inner value. I have made mistakes. I pray my daughters will do better for themselves. Perhaps you can avoid some of the pain and emptiness that I have brought upon myself.

You may try to ignore evaluating how important your professional life is compared with your personal life. But you will always be reacting and catching up to the inherent vagaries of life. You will always find yourself buffeted around in a whirlwind of chaos. You may end up living a life whose major cornerstones are guilt, stress, and resentment. Think about it. That is what I am doing as I type the pages of this book—for the first time, maybe in my life, I am stopping and asking: What is my true value? What "profits" will I be left with after all is said and done? What will be my legacy?

You can criticize yourself endlessly. Or you can grow your value. You can decide to strategically, confidently maneuver your life in the direction you choose—the direction that reflects your goals. To the extent that her many roles blend—and even fuse—a woman can say that she truly feels success-ful. I honestly don't believe that as working women, spouses, and mothers, we should be condemned to live two completely separate lives, juggling multiple personalities that leave us feeling crazy and exhausted. Some incredibly powerful women disagree with me, so I will lay out all sides of this conversation, and you will decide what is best for you.

I sometimes think that if our lives could be mapped, they would look like Venn diagrams, those charts that illustrate the connections between different groups by assigning circles to them and showing how those circles intercept each other—or, in some cases, not at all. In the case of our lives as working women, the circles represent our overall identity and dreams. We can create a map that looks like a night sky with densely packed constellations of circles in one area and with other circles floating completely on their own, like orphan planets. Or the circles on our map can overlap so closely that our Venn diagram looks like a picture of a world.

The question is: How can we get them to overlap more seamlessly? In the following chapters we're going to find out.

CHAPTER TWO

DEFINING YOUR PROFESSIONAL VALUE AND SPEAKING UP FOR YOURSELF

Whearen I'm dressing for work, I check my reflection to make sure that everything is where it's supposed to be. Often I see two Mikas. No, my closet doesn't have twin mirrors, and I haven't forgotten my glasses. (I actually have terrible vision and desperately need to get to my eye doctor—maybe after this book!) The reason I see double is because there are two versions of me that walk out into the world every day—and I have spent my entire adult life learning about the value of each of them while wishing they were one and the same.

I'm a slow learner. It took me years before I fathomed that my professional self and personal self were genuinely different from each other. It was longer still before I came to understand that each was equally important, even if the balance tipped from day to day, year to year. Then I spent another eight years gradually identifying, evaluating, cultivating, and knowing my financial worth during the rebirth of my career in television news, when I joined Joe Scarborough as cohost of *Morning Joe*.

It's only now that I fully appreciate that the only way for me to feel like a successful woman is to grow my value in all areas of my life. It took me roughly three decades to get all this, but it doesn't have to take you anywhere near that long. I'm not saying that experience and accumulated wisdom aren't important, because they absolutely are. But you don't have to waste time. If you want to feel like a truly successful woman, you *shouldn't* waste time. You can learn to define—and expand the definitions of—your professional and personal identities now.

To do that, we're going to go on a little tour. Of you. You're going to take a really hard look at your professional self and your private self. You're going to remember the moment you entered adult public life—for most of us, that happened when we got our first real job—because it was within that first minute that you began to develop a professional persona distinct from your personal identity. You're going to think about the enormity of that growth spurt and whether you were conscious of it then or if you are even now. Even so, you did it. You demarcated two states of being in yourself: one, to adjust and rise to the demands and conditions of your new professional life, and the other, to establish your new adult personal life and settle into what you were really feeling inside. You're going to pinpoint the degree to which you are in control—really in the conductor's seat—and the degree to which you have, consciously or not, allowed circumstances to dictate your life's direction.

If you've never thought about any of this explicitly, don't worry—that's completely normal. The development of your professional persona probably occurred so naturally, so gradually, that you probably didn't even notice that it was happening.

What I want you to do right now is to notice. Take inventory. Of all of it.

THE BIRTH OF YOUR PROFESSIONAL PERSONA

Let's talk about the Big Bang of your career: the birth of your professional persona. When you entered the workplace as a young adult, it was probably the first time you'd ever had to behave in a way different from just yourself—however cool, quirky, smart, bubbly, or however you'd wanted to come across to your friends in school or college (we've all been there). Moreover, if you were in your early twenties and just coming out of college, it was probably the first time you'd ever not been a student. And on the path to knowing your professional marketability, the experience of graduating from being a student to a working person is a major landmark.

After all, in college you had enormous control over the scale and scope of your own success, as well as a great deal of freedom to decide the particular areas at which you actively wanted to succeed. It was all in your lap. There were clear instructions on how to achieve, and everyone knew them, from deans and professors to students: study the material, participate in class, and perform well on graded work. That was pretty much the blueprint, and to the extent that you followed it, your sense of value as a student was either elevated or deflated. The particular nature of your interests and aptitude became even more finely honed once you chose a major. No matter how diligent you were or weren't, you were making your first important declaration of your interests and your abilities. In short, it was the first time you really asserted your sense of who you were as a young adult.

Then you graduated. You entered the workforce. And your sense of self and exactly what it is you have to offer probably vaporized on contact.

That's basically what happened to me. I had been an English major in college, and a pretty decent one—I thought. But when I was applying for jobs at local television news stations, the producers didn't care that I'd been a hard-working student or that I had graduated from Williams College. And the competition for even the smallest television markets in the country was brutal. I was darn lucky just to land a job helping staff reporters and producers track down whether oil spills on the highway or fender benders in the suburbs were worth pursuing as TV news stories. But deploying my student's sense of value in this field? Are you kidding? What did parsing a Shakespeare sonnet have to do with a breech at a local sewage treatment plant? What did Jane Austen have to do with a homicide in Hartford?

The skills I had learned in college were seemingly use-less—and my sense of my own value plummeted. As I wrote in my first book, *All Things at Once*: "I'd wanted to be actively engaged in building my career, and laying the foundation for a family—and I was nowhere. . . . To borrow a line from Pat Buchanan that he shared one day on *Morning Joe*, I felt like 'a big nothing burger.'"

I also had no real mentor; no boss who was going to show me the ropes. I had to figure everything out on the fly. Is that striking a familiar chime with you? It happens to many of us. After having been hired, you're given a job title, but, depending on how lucky you are in your boss, either you are given thorough training or someone who just basically tosses a stack of papers on your desk and says, "Organize and file," before vanishing into a labyrinth of beige cubicles. Where is the blueprint to succeed like the one you had in college? A human resources staffer might have given you an employee handbook covering health benefits and antidis-crimination policies on your first day, but there are no instruc-tions on how to excel at this job. You have to wing it. On your own.

And thus your professional identity is born: the personal-ity you wear at work. But this game face isn't good enough. Straight up: your career will not become as successful as it can be unless you can grow that professional persona into some-thing much bigger and more valuable. Indeed, it becomes the basis for your professional value: that unique set of personal qualities, professional style, and work experience that sets you apart from everyone else in the room.

PROFESSIONAL VALUE–BUILDING BASICS

Developing your professional brand, one that has financial value, is different from just doing a good job at work. It's about developing a skill set that you can translate into a brand. You need to be patient. This will take time to evolve and mature. First, you have to earn your chops. You need to put in your time doing the kind of drudgery that has attended every entry-level job in the history of employment. But by bearing down and doing it, you learn how to do hard work and probably work you don't like to do—and it also burns off any residual collegiate arrogance. This isn't college anymore.

At work you build a new sense of value. You learn how to act—and how not to act—with everyone at your organization, from your boss to the executive-in-chief to your peers. You learn how to dress appropriately. You learn what your place is and how to maximize it so you can move on to the next place you'd like to go. You come to understand how the system and politics of your workplace operate. You make mistakes, and you learn how to handle them and how those mistakes impact your sense of professional value. Same thing with your successes: you observe how successful people a rung—or more—above you do their jobs, watching their wins and their flops and learning about how the pros get work done.

One of my most important mentors early on would turn out to be my future husband, Jim. We met in our early twenties, working together at a small Fox station in Hartford, Connecticut. He was thorough, tireless, and always naturally connected with whomever he was interviewing. He had a brand as the best reporter in the market. It was a hard-fought reputation. Looking at how good he was as an investigative reporter, I realized that it would take years for me to reach that level of expertise.

Jim was and still is candid with me about my work. After the first break of my career, covering a double homicide in the Stowe Village public housing projects in a miniskirt and heels in the middle of winter (basically, looking every bit the spoiled, uptight white girl in a throng of people who were not happy to have me on their home turf), Jim told me I'd done "a nice job." Not criticism, but not exactly overwhelming praise either—nor did I deserve any. The next time I was more prepared. I dressed appropriately, I was ready, and I was confident. It was the start of my career in television journalism.

All of these first work experiences—whether they're two years' worth or twenty—are the seeds you plant to grow your brand and increase its worth. Therefore, it's important to reflect on them, think about what you learned from them, and choose which parts you want to nurture and grow. If you're the journaling type, then journal away. If you're more of a list maker, use an outline or make bullet points. If you're reentering work life after staying home with your children for a few (or more) years, it's a good time to regroup and plot out your career strategy. Keep track of what you enjoy and strategize how to do more of it. You can even ask your kids to help you make a PowerPoint presentation. I don't care how you do it; just give your work and life journey real thought. Make the connections between how one move or observation led to the next, positive or negative, and where it took you. It's time to start mapping out your professional value: the amalgamation of all your experiences and assets that make you vital on the job.

Take, for example, the experience of television senior executive, producer, and impresario Nely Galán, the former head of Telemundo, the largest Spanish-speaking television company in the world, and self-styled "Latina Tyler Perry." When you speak with her it's clear that Nely is absolutely positive—in every sense of the word—about her professional value. "My professional value is about being fully and authentically Latina, and yet a Latina who can be fully in the mainstream. Which I think is the quagmire of Latina women in America, just like many different women around the world— Middle Eastern women, Indian women, Chinese women— who come from traditional cultures," she said, talking about her own professional value from her home in Venice Beach, California. "We seem to always be in the crossroads of fully being authentic to our traditions, but we want to be part of the mainstream too. So I think I built a profession in the first part of my life around television, telling the stories of those women at the crossroads."

And how did she develop her professional value? What about her past prepared her to build it? Where did it come from in her life? "I was born in Cuba. We immigrated to this country when I was five. My parents were very Latino and very proud to be Latino, and always made me feel that being Latina was the best of both worlds. And I really always felt that—which I think is important for me to say to other women from other cultures. I always felt like I would make double the money because I knew two cultures really well," she said, speaking about how her upbringing shaped from an early age her clear sense of herself professionally and personally. "[I always knew] whatever I did, I would bring my two sides. And I always say that I could be a million things. I don't think it's all about this one career. It's more about finding your voice. Like, if I was a doctor, I would be helping Latinos and I'd also be fully in the mainstream, publishing and being a doctor. . . . If I was a lawyer, I'd probably be in some way helping Latinos, and maybe not even charging Latinos and taking on very high-end clients to pay for my practice. If I'm a teacher, I would be focused a lot on Latino kids. . . . I concerned myself more about what was my voice, what was my authentic voice, than what specific career I was going to go into. Because it didn't really matter. I was going to be successful at anything I did."

Nely's upbringing didn't play a coincidental role in her professional life—indeed, it shaped her professional value. How does your background shape yours? How did the way you were raised give you a special perspective—on what? Was there a moment in your upbringing that marked a turning point for you, when you had an inkling or outright decided what you wanted to do for a living when you "grew up"?

FOUND MY FOOTING

Let's look at your early work history. Think back. There is usually a story—more specifically, your own personal story—that illustrates the moment you first had your "Wow, I've arrived!" experience on the job. That story tells you a lot about the origins of your professional value. For Nancy Gibbs, managing editor of *TIME*, it was getting an assignment she didn't want. "Back around 1988 the editor of *TIME*, Henry Muller, called me to his office to tell me that I had passed the 'writer's trial' given to fact checkers who hoped to be promoted," Nancy wrote to me. "But now, Henry told me, I was a full-fledged staff writer. I was elated. And, he went on, henceforth I was no longer assigned to the International section; I was to be the new Living writer, reporting to a legendary and notoriously rigorous editor named Martha Duffy, one of the first women ever to hold that title at *TIME*. I was crushed. I gulped my thanks, left Henry's office, and went back to see my great mentor Otto Friedrich. 'I don't want to be the Living writer,' I told him. 'Living stories are about ice cream flavors and designer dogs. I hate the Living section!' And he just smiled at me and said, 'Nancy. . . . this is the best thing that ever could have happened. Everyone hates the Living section. This is your chance to do whatever you want with it. And Martha wouldn't have asked for you if she didn't think you could do it.'

"So one of my first Living cover stories was about a landmark Supreme Court case concerning the right to die. I wrote about date rape when that phrase was brand new; about how we apportion resources between children and the elderly; about crime and punishment, faith and values, politics, policy. Martha, who was famous for not suffering fools, was a great editor and champion, and subsequent editors kept letting me try new things, search for the story that doesn't fall into a category, for which I am forever grateful. The next *TIME* editor, Jim Gaines, a terrific journalist with a great story sense, started assigning me the cover story every third or fourth week. And he gave me a raise I hadn't asked for. That was when I had a sense I might have found my footing."

After surviving that proving ground—and prevailing—Nancy's professional value began to solidify. "I used to say it came down to the central rule of news writers: you have to write faster than everyone who writes better, and better than everyone who writes faster," she mused. "I have since come to think of it as patrolling the territory where public and private intersect, on both the What and the Why of major events, which is how I came to focus in my books as well as my journalism on the presidency. I'm not just interested in what presidents do in the job; I want to know what the job does to them."

Very clear. Honed by her experience. Realizes what her unique perspective is. Nancy knows exactly what she brings to the table—her capabilities, her talents, and her value in the marketplace. She took smart, calculated risks that she knew would make her job more interesting to her and that she hoped would improve the magazine. It worked, and now she's in charge of the place.

Michele Sullivan, the first woman president of the Caterpillar Foundation, the philanthropic arm of the heavy construction equipment behemoth, is also clear on her mission. As the head of an international nonprofit, she has decided that it will, in large part, focus on improving the lives of girls and women in high-needs circumstances. "In Africa boys go to school. The girls look for water all day and don't go to school. When you then provide them with water—a well or a hookup—if it's in India, for example, the girls now have a chance to go to school and become educated. And it's totally putting them on the path to prosperity," Michele explained to me when I invited her on as a guest on *Morning Joe*. "But even in the US we are investing in organizations such as LISC, the Local Initiative Support Corporation, which is well known for turning around impoverished neighborhoods. We opened an office in Peoria, Illinois, which is the world headquarters of Caterpillar. And we just opened the first financial opportunity center right in an impoverished neighborhood, which gives an integrated approach to the families. They budget, they learn about their credit score, they get ready for a job, and most of the clients are single women. So when you start to put your money in the women and the girls, the family will start to flourish."

Michele's mission for the Caterpillar Foundation and the brand it represents are tied together. Moreover, she's tied herself and her own sense of inner value to that brand. As a little person, Michele has overcome many of her own personal hurdles at work and in her personal life. She wants the Caterpillar Foundation to give to other women what she feels so blessed to have had. "I know how lucky I am in so many ways. People don't have what I have, but they should. A woman should have self-esteem. If a woman has self-esteem, she has everything to start," she said to me. "And I've always had that, thanks to my parents and where I was born. Not everybody has that. And that's where it comes from in me."

The cosmetics queen and mogul Bobbi Brown is also clear on her brand—not just for her line of makeup but also for the philosophy behind it, the one that drives her as a business-woman, wife, and mother. "I certainly believe that confidence is the secret to beauty. Self-esteem is how you feel about your-self. If you compare yourself to women whom you meet or actresses on television—supermodels for sure—you don't usu-ally win those kinds of contests. But if you look inside yourself and you learn to love who you are and enhance your features, then you become your best self. My motto is 'Be who you are,'" she told me during a conversation we had for this book. "We don't do makeovers at our counter; we do lessons. We teach women how to do their makeup in their style, and that's been a really big, important part of our growth."

How does she see her professional value, if it could be reduced to a few sentences? "I think I am simple. I am straight-forward. I am honest. I have a little bit of a wicked sense of humor and a funny wit. And I believe in telling the truth," Bobbi said to me. That core piece of her professional value is reflected, she told me, in her cosmetics brand as well. "I, like most of the women who come to my counter, am usually multitasking. You know, many of us have husbands, children, jobs, things that we volunteer for, and we get overloaded. We need something quick and easy. So I understand really strongly that for most of us women, we need things that are simple, quick, and actually do what they promise to do."

Building your professional value isn't an overnight job, and it isn't easy. You have to be bold. Ask yourself tough questions and give real answers.

- What about my background has shaped what I am doing now? What about it is shaping what I want to do?
- How has each of my experiences built on the last?
- What was my pivotal work experience that told me that I was really thriving?
- What were my biggest three mistakes and what did I learn from them—and what about my behavior still holds me back?
- What have my biggest three successes taught me about what I'm good at and what I love doing?
- What characteristics have earned me positive attention at work?
- Which of my personality traits have earned me lukewarm or negative attention?
- What do I want to accomplish in my life? What do I *need* to accomplish?
- What haven't I done but am dying to try?

Try it. Learn what dreams and goals are lurking in your psyche. Take time pulling them out and admiring them from different angles. Get inspired. Get driven. Get action oriented. Just don't take as much time as I did. As Nely was told on a trip by a group of eighty-something-year-old fellow travelers: "'Honey, do everything on your bucket list before you're sixty-five. Because after you're sixty-five, your body is a ticking time bomb.'"

JILL OF ALL TRADES

For the first twenty years of my career as a television news journalist, I had no professional value. The concept never even occurred to me. In the early years I had a ridiculous stereotype of a television news reporter in my head, and I overdressed and overacted for the part—marking me as a rank amateur, although I didn't know it at the time. Even when I started dressing more conservatively—though with zero personal style—for years, I had, a rather amorphous professional persona. My response to not being shown how to do my job— to build my professional value—was to become a Jill of All Trades. I surfed through my career, riding wave after wave, a combination of the ebb and flow of the relentless news business and my compulsive reactivity to it. I was willing to do— and did do—whatever the newsroom producers needed done: cover local crises, read the evening news, and so forth.

At age thirty I was the anchor of CBS's *Up to the Minute*, which taped at nine o'clock at night and then shot live from a grueling two o'clock in the morning until five. It was a thankless job, and in truth, I hated it. I was so worn ragged from the punishing hours that one night, barely conscious, I fell down the stairs at home while carrying my infant daughter, Carlie, and risked both of our lives. It was nothing short of a miracle that we ended up being fine ultimately, but not without Carlie breaking a leg and me suffering from near-paralyzing guilt that I still haven't been able to let go of. Still, I did that job because I was young and wanted that work experience. In hindsight I realize that I needed to learn what I liked doing and where I wanted to take it. I needed to start building my professional value.

But I didn't. I continued to run wherever I was told to go. Now, some of those experiences were incredibly enriching. I had a front-row seat to history, as it happened. For example, I reported on up-to-the-minute chad counting during the infamous Bush-Gore election of 2000 for MSNBC, and I all but lived at the Secaucus, New Jersey, studios for that tense and unexpectedly protracted period of time. I reported from a dangerously blown-out outpost, steps away from the World Trade Center on September 11, 2001, and became CBS's voice from Ground Zero. I participated in some major moments in the early part of American twenty-first-century history, and I'm proud of my work.

I also wore pencil skirts, fabulous boots, and, along with my two female cohosts, bubbled a daily girlish "Shoe check!" as we stuck out our bedecked feet to gush over in mutual admiration, all for the women's cable show *HomePage*, which *Entertainment Weekly*, probably rightly, dubbed "*The PowerPuff Girls* of journalism." They asked, and I delivered.

I had done a lot of different things, but I had no focus. I was constantly reacting to what was needed instead of proactively pitching stories that had my particular perspective or stamp branded into them. Truthfully I didn't think of pitching any of those stories because I didn't have an area of expertise. I didn't think of myself as being the one in control—

I was there to please my superiors. I did what I was told to do. Or I pitched what I thought *they* would like, not what interested me.

What I considered the height of my career was in my mid- to late thirties when I reported for *CBS Sunday Morning,* the *CBS Evening News, 48 Hours,* and *60 Minutes II.* The producers assigned me stories, and I thought I had arrived because I was always overbooked. I was busy, but I was definitely *not* in the conductor's seat; I was more like a very eager passenger. I thought I was doing the right thing by making myself indispensable, the kind of reporter whom producers would send out on any story because they knew I was up for and equal to the job. I had that professional reputation to the extent that people in the newsroom teased me for being Overbooked Mika.

Still, after twenty years in the business, I had no immediately identifiable brand, nothing that distinguished me as an instantly recognizable television personality known for her perspective, professionalism, and personal style. In short, I had no professional value. And that's why, I believe, I was ultimately fired from CBS, the last job I had before joining MSNBC's *Morning Joe* in 2007. With a new president then at the helm, there was a "housecleaning." I was easy to lose. Although I would do anything, to the higher-ups I represented nothing in particular. Instead of being indispensable, I had made myself easily disposable. Because there was nothing unique that I brought to the table—nothing that I could articulate, anyway—that reflected my own professional value. I could be replaced by anyone willing and able to do the jobs I had done. And I was.

LUCKY JUST TO BE AT THE TABLE

Blair Blackwell knows this story all too well. Now manager of Education and Corporate Programs at Chevron, Blair had been frustrated at a nonprofit for years, somehow unable to carve out a role to be where she could shine. Ultimately she left her job and spent eight months interviewing people she trusted, reading and networking in order to find a meaningful position that afforded upward growth and opportunity.

When she read *Knowing Your Value*, Blair had her "aha" moment. She instantly recognized that her reticence to advocate for herself had kept her from reaching her potential at work. "I was always overly accommodating," Blair said. "I felt lucky just to be at the table rather than having an attitude of 'I'm the right person to be at this table.'" Just as I had been, Blair was a "yes" woman, willing to do whatever was asked of her even though her experience and performance were manifest proof that she was capable of far more. She hadn't fully recognized—and she certainly hadn't communicated—her professional value. She hadn't spoken up. And because of that, she wasn't heard.

So Blair took time to consider carefully her next move. Her career included stints as a tax consultant, education adviser, and development director in places as diverse as Kazakhstan, Bosnia, and New York, and Blair knew she had to step up her game in articulating the skills she offered. When she spread out the diverse assortment of jobs on her résumé, she worried that to others it looked as if she lacked focus. But as she looked more closely she noticed that the amazing variety had informed her work life. "I've invested a lot of time learning from my career successes as well as the challenges or frustrations I've faced," she said. "[Reading] *Knowing Your Value* gave me permission to not be perfect and to better appreciate all that my varied experience brings to the table. That's pretty powerful. So when I was in my job discussions with Chevron, I had more confidence articulating my experience and value and asking for the salary commensurate with that. I'm now in a position I love and in a place in which I feel extremely respected and empowered."

That's a major element of not just knowing but also growing your professional value: you must articulate it clearly, be a strong advocate for yourself, and allow your personality to shine boldly. Noticeably. I can't stress that enough. Blair had not effectively done that, she said, until she had read my book. Why not? I wondered, as I often do about myself and the many women I meet who have been or are in Blair's (and my) shoes. What did she think had been holding her back—psychologically—from marketing her professional value at work? Blair admitted that she had probably unconsciously been too afraid to promote herself because, she said, she didn't want to appear "aggressive."

AMBITIOUS WOMEN ARE ATTRACTIVE

Okay, let's just stop here for a minute and clear something up. There is a toxic sexist stereotype that's been floating around in our culture's well water for far too long. I think it's time we filter out the concept that "aggressive" women are unattractive.

This is just wrong. So-called aggressive women, to me, are those who know their value, speak up for themselves, and offer their perspective where pertinent. They are leaders. From where I sit, aggressive women are crucial in a business setting. These women often get what they want because they have the confidence to speak up. It's almost as simple as that.

Let me tell you one of my favorite aggressive woman stories. I was in the Milly boutique in Manhattan (Michelle Smith, founder of the Milly label, is one of my all-time favorite designers, and you'll meet this imaginative, successful, and resilient woman later in the book). While I was shopping, a young woman approached me with a beautiful, welcoming smile. With personal poise and genuine graciousness, she told me how much she loved the show and that as an up-and-coming shoe designer, she *really* loved my fashion sense—the way I wore my shoes, in particular, was flat-out hot and classically tasteful all at once. Would I accept a pair of boots that she had designed, that she was sure that I would love?

I couldn't say, "Are you kidding me? Yes!" fast enough. And I had no idea of what these boots even looked like yet. But I was almost positive that I was going to love them simply because of the way she had presented herself to me. In the less than two minutes it took for her to introduce herself as Layla-Joy Williams, she had impressed me with lovely manners, a warm confidence, and her outfit, which was a flawless communication of what I would call elegant bohemian—ebullient and artsy yet neatly pulled together and sophisticated.

There was no question that this was an aggressive, ambitious young woman; after all, she'd marched right up and boldly pushed her product line on me, obviously hoping I'd wear her boots on air so that she could get free, national publicity. She knew exactly what she was doing. But the truth is that a lot of people hustle their stuff at me for the exact same purpose. But generally they are either offensive, rude, and cocky; too meek to make their point quickly and effectively; or so slavishly flattering that their obvious insincerity only makes me feel used and squeamish. Layla-Joy Williams, however, had the whole package, and that signaled to me a core competence: my instinct told me that she was going to be successful because of that.

I happily took her card and the boots, which I loved so much that I wore them at the shoot for my *Cosmo* column (which means that Layla-Joy's boots are now featured in one of the top women's magazines every month). She has become one of my fashion contacts and unofficial mentees—young women I've taken an interest in and introduce to key players who I think will be helpful to them as they start their careers.

Another one of my favorite aggressive women stories involves meeting Allison Dorst, founder and head of the athletic fashion site Pinks and Greens. Allison approached me in an elevator when I was rushing between two events, effectively pitching her company—stylish workout clothes that actually fit and flatter women of all body types—to me in just under two minutes. By minute three she had my personal e-mail address.

Alison followed up with me over e-mail consistently, for over two months, until I had the time to bring her in to 30 Rock for a meeting. When she got the chance, she came prepared. Allison walked into my office with samples of her merchandise and a clear vision of her brand's potential. When I asked her whether she could come back again the next day, she did, no questions asked. Frankly I admired her spunk, tenacity, and fearlessness right from the very beginning—so much so that I ultimately became an investor in her company and brought her on to help with my Know Your Value events, starting with that very first one in Hartford. Who better to help me with an "elevator pitch" competition than the woman who actually pitched me in an elevator? We now have a relationship that is mutually beneficial, all because Alison came ready to play. She's aggressive, for sure—shy types don't corner people in elevators—just one of the reasons I know her company is going to be wildly successful.

But let's face it: most people just don't like the term "aggressive." And when someone uses adjectives like "aggressive" and "unattractive" to describe a woman's professional behavior, we all intuitively grasp the subtext. Such comments are made to remind us, subtly or not, that we are there to err on the side of "talk nice and look pretty." Essentially, to be people-pleasers. So if you don't like the word "aggressive," substitute one that you identify with: ambitious, determined, focused, assertive, direct. Whatever term we use, we must stop letting the fear of powerful characteristics being attributed to us get in the way of making the most of our careers. Certainly personal style, dignity, sense of humor, and strong work ethic are welcome qualities at any job. But being nervous about being seen as "unattractive" for promoting your accomplishments in the right place at the right time? Please.

Getting back to "aggressive," I have to admit that I like the term and all that it connotes. It's a word I'd like to see powerful women take back, own for themselves, and use to define and grow their professional value. Yet it's complicated and controversial, especially when it comes to power dynamics between men and women in the workplace.

But why is that? When I was meeting up with my friend, cosmetics mogul Bobbi Brown, I knew she'd be the perfect person to help me think this through. After all, if anyone knows about being successful and attractive, it's Bobbi. It's the basis of her entire business; in fact, the tagline of her company's philosophy is, "Pretty Powerful." So I asked for her nuanced response as to why the word "aggressive" to describe successful professional women was so problematic.

Bobbi was thoughtful. I could tell she didn't completely like the word. "I think the word I would choose to use is being 'fearless,'" she said. "A lot of people are afraid of doing the wrong thing. . . . I think the difference is being assertive is one thing, being aggressive is not positive." Not positive? Why is aggression such a bad thing—and is it only considered so when it applies to women? "'Aggression' is not positive because, to me, that comes with intensity and anger," she explained. "I think just being 'assertive' but mostly just not being afraid [is what has worked for me]." I ran another laden term by her. What about the word "ambitious"? Did she like that way of describing the same kind of powerful women? "I think 'ambitious' is great," she raved. "It's passion, it's drive, it's hard work. People forget about the words 'hard work.' Hard work is really the most important thing."

Bobbi is right, of course. Hard work is absolutely the most important thing a person can contribute to her career. And if you want to be successful, you have to take it for granted that hard work is going to dominate your work life. But there's a little trick to it. Hard work on the job is a little like the tree falling in the forest: it doesn't make much noise if no one hears about it.

So for heaven's sake, speak up. If I hadn't spoken up about why I needed a raise on *Morning Joe*—especially when Joe was making fourteen times what I was making—I might still be making a day rate as a freelancer on the show. And by the way, I had to be "aggressive" about it. If I hadn't communicated my value in a direct, unapologetic way, who would have paid me what I am worth? Advocating for yourself is simply what a competitive workplace demands. In fact, it's expected. If you don't proactively endorse yourself and your work, chances are you aren't going to get very far.

YOUR BOSS HAS NO MEMORY

In my three decades of working in ferociously competitive environments, I've realized that men know that the above statement about bosses is true. Have you ever met a successful man in any workplace who doesn't make sure he gets credit for everything he's had a hand in doing? Unless you work for a religious institution or place of worship, my guess is that you haven't.

This is not usually the case with women. In talking with women all around the country I have found that many simply assume that their good work is being noticed, noted, and filed away in consideration for future promotions. This is simply not true. Not by a long shot. Every workplace is busy, no matter what kind it is. Your superiors have a lot on their minds, and much of the time they're likely racing to stay just ahead of the curve so that the people they answer to don't steamroll them.

So commit this to memory right now, verbatim: your boss probably has no memory at all of the great work you have done. That's why, even with a solid track record, you must be assertive (or fill in the blank with your adjective of choice). You must check in with your higher-ups to explain exactly why you are the perfect person for the new job, the raise, flextime—whatever you need. This behavior isn't merely appropriate; it's essential to growing your professional value and to your career overall. If, for example, you have pulled off profitable projects that were made better by your particular handling of them and you can make the case for yourself— that is, you can really articulate your professional value—I am confident that you'll get what you want. Or at least you'll get more than what you had when you first walked in the office. Consider the following three scenarios.

In Scenario A, Mika works like crazy for every news show her network produces, but she never lets the president know how much and what kind of work she's doing, or how these accomplishments raise the profile of the company. Because no one knows what precisely she brings to the table or how to best steer her talents and energy, Mika is one of the first to go when trimming needs to be done in the department (as indeed I was).

In Scenario B, Mika starts a new job. When she does exceedingly well and believes she deserves a raise commensurate with her worth to the company, she tries to act like a guy (like Joe). She trash-talks to her boss about getting more money and even jabs him in the shoulder because she thinks she's required to act like a man to get a salary equal to a man's. But her efforts are seen as shrill, bizarre, and completely out of character, so her request is ignored.

In Scenario C, however, Mika finally gets smart. She books time with her boss (after enough time has passed after the "guy" negotiation) and tells him exactly why he needs to compensate her. She also explains why the company is not doing right by her, because her value is far greater than its estimation. Her boss listens to her frank appraisal of her own past and continued contributions to the show—which, by the way, is on the serious upswing. This is in part because not only is she the perfect sidekick, but she also handles a very live, nonscripted, politically focused television show with smarts, humor, poise, and relatability. These qualities draw a much wider swath of viewers than the show would otherwise have. Mika is also willing to show him, in no uncertain terms, what the show looks like without her. She is ready to walk.

She has figured out a plan B, so her negotiating position is strong.

The boss concedes her points and agrees to "fix" the problem. Mika doesn't end up getting a salary that's at parity with her male counterpart, but she gets a boost significant enough to satisfy her that she is getting paid within the ballpark of her value. It's a happy ending—and it's all true.

Adapt Scenario C's script to your own position, coming up with your own lines. If what you're saying is true and you have put in the hard work, I can all but guarantee that you will get the attention and respect of your superiors. Because here's the reality: people who are able to market their professional value effectively are seen, consciously or not, as go-getters, the kinds of employees who are going to run with an assignment, bring fresh insights to it, and work like crazy on it. They are seen as dynamic workers who might draw more business into the organization. That's the kind of person whom superiors want to hire and promote.

People-pleasers, however, consciously or not, are seen as rather like puppies. They're game and full of energy, and they like to do what's asked of them. But they also seem just kind of, well, spazzy and erratic. They seem to have no sense of themselves and what they uniquely bring to the table. They seem to have no vision or direction; they're so driven by the fear of being disliked that they don't stand out enough for anyone important to notice them. Ultimately people-pleasers are the most replaceable. Don't be one. (And, no, this is not the last time I'm going to remind you.)

WHO YOU ARE AND WHAT YOU WANT

A major part of growing your worth—and of using it to your best advantage at work—is continuing to interview yourself, asking ever tougher and tougher questions. By answering key questions, you will know how to pitch your strengths powerfully in the marketplace and identify and articulate your own defining goals in life. In short, you will know who you are— and what you want.

So ask and answer:

- What strong traits do I have that I've undersold or hidden? (My example: ambitious, focused, energetic (possibly supersonically), competitive, direct.)
- If I was going to write a fifteen-word ad for myself, what would it say? (My example: "She's smart. She's direct. She's funny. She's informed. All this and fabulous too.")
- What do I *not* want my professional persona to be? (My example: People-pleasing workaholic with no clear boundaries or particular perspective.)
- What can I do in the future to avoid self-damaging behavior in the office? My examples:

1) **PROBLEM:** Stop being overly emotional. FIX: Don't initiate important conversations or meetings, or reschedule them if I'm feeling intense.

2) **PROBLEM:** Stop making self-flagellating comments at work. FIX: Appropriately self-deprecating is one thing; horsehair shirts are self-destructive, inappropriate, and make people uncomfortable.

3) **PROBLEM:** Stop letting others take credit for my work/ideas. FIX: Speak up when this happens—that is, "I'm so glad that you agree with that point—that's exactly why I brought it up a few weeks ago at our meeting." Own it. Say it.

If I had to sum up my professional value in one sentence, what would it be? (My example: See next paragraph!)

After a lifetime of work experience, eight years as cohost of *Morning Joe*, and now as an advocate for women knowing and growing their value, this is mine. I am Mika Brzezinski, cohost of MSNBC's *Morning Joe* and three-time *New York Times* best-selling author. I am focused, determined, smart—always ready for a spontaneous quip, verbal volley, and laugh, or to deploy the smooth political segue when tense moments erupt on set and in public life.

Ask what I bring to the table, and I can tell you in one sentence: "Mika Brzezinski is a career television journalist with three decades of news and anchor reporting, who is building a movement to help all women grow their value in their careers and their lives."

That's it. That's my professional value.

But the Mika who is wife, mother, daughter, sister, and friend? That's a different story. That Mika is learning to quantify her inner value. And so will you. We're going to search for and find ways to grow both the professional and personal aspects of your import and impact as a person. In this way you can be the woman, professional, friend—perhaps wife and mother—that you want to be. We're going to become *truly* successful.

CHAPTER THREE

KNOWING YOUR INNER VALUE

A little more than a year ago I was on an airplane going back to New York after a book event in Washington State. It was a late afternoon flight, but unless you're taking a red-eye, it doesn't matter: when you fly from west to east, you're almost always riding into darkness. I had worked fourteen-hour days out west, and I wanted nothing more than to do what everyone else around me was doing—curl up with a fleece airline blanket and take a nap. But I couldn't. My daughter Emilie had begun the process of applying to colleges, a process I'd really wanted to be a part of. In my carry-on bag I had a big folder with her brag sheets, stories, and summer-reading essays. I thought I'd review her writing style so I could be more helpful when we filled out all those applications.

One essay was on *Into the Wild*, the work of narrative nonfiction about a young man a few years older than Emilie who had essentially disappeared after graduating from college to live in nature. Ultimately he was found dead, alone, from starvation in Alaska. In the essay students were asked whether they would have been able to do what the main character, the self-named "Alexander Supertramp," had done: abandon their families and lives to do something they really believed in. They were also asked who they would miss the most.

I read my daughter's beautifully written essay that explained, no, she would not be able to do what Alexander Supertramp had done—she would miss her dad too much. She worried about her father, she said, because he was home alone a good deal of the time, and she wouldn't be able to leave for fear of making him lonely.

There I was, listening to the hum of the plane, everyone else asleep. I burst into tears. I was proud of her. It was an articulate, really caring piece of writing. I felt the closeness she had with her dad. I was reading about my family. The one that was happening without me.

UP AGAINST IT

Back then, I felt as though my own soul had gone into the wild, alone. What had happened to me? What had happened to my daughter? To my husband? With all my focus on knowing my professional brand, what had happened to any sense of inner value? As wife, mother—even friend and daughter—was my innermost sense of who I was being neglected? I looked at the businessman sprawled in the aisle seat across from me. He had a wedding ring on. His chair was reclined back, and he was asleep with his mouth wide open. Do men feel this way when they travel for work? I wondered.

I don't think these questions are uncommon. We women often ask ourselves how we can be fulfilled in all areas of our lives. But when we talk about our successes as working women, we spend so much time describing professional obligations and achievements that we miss the boat. The challenges we face along the way are not just professional; we have to admit that they're personal too.

For some very successful women the gap between their professional value and their inner value—what really matters to us as people, beyond work—is simply a nonissue. *TIME*'s Nancy Gibbs, for one, seems to have found a way to seal up that crevasse. "Starting even before my daughters were born, I turned down promotions when they would have meant doing a job I didn't think I would be good at or happy doing. I've loved being a writer; loved the flexibility, the creativity, the autonomy, and felt hugely blessed that my role at *TIME* allowed that flexibility, especially when our daughters were little," she wrote to me. "I think if you are responsible for producing a product, whether a piece of writing or anything else, you can have enormous freedom so long as you meet your deadlines and maintain your standards."

For fashion designer Tory Burch the distinction between her professional life and inner values are clear, and the two came to coexist happily. "I had worked in the fashion industry for many years, doing PR and marketing first at Ralph

Lauren, then at Vera Wang, and then working for Narciso Rodriguez at Loewe. While at Loewe I was offered the job of president at about the same time that I learned I was pregnant with my third son. I knew I couldn't do that job and be the kind of mom I wanted to be, so I decided to take some time off to focus on my family," she responded when I asked her to talk about how she negotiated her sense of worth as a working woman as well as a wife, mother, and human being.

"It was a tough decision. Having a career was incredibly important to me, and I knew it would be a challenge to come back. But having a family was paramount. I also knew at some point I would have to find a way to balance both. It was during that time that I began developing the concept for our company." I asked Tory how she would characterize her personal priorities—her inner value. "I am the working mother of three boys, and they come first no matter what. I take them to school in the morning, and I make it home in time for dinner most evenings, even if it means having a meeting in the car on the way to my apartment."

The comedienne and actress Susie Essman, who plays the hilarious, potty-mouthed wife of Larry David's agent on *Curb Your Enthusiasm*, is another woman who has found peace with her outer and inner lives. Actually she's done far better than that. Susie has essentially made a career—built her professional value—out of her MO. "I would say my professional value [is] not caring what people think . . . otherwise I wouldn't be able to say the things that I say," she said to Joe and me one morning on the set. "I think that women are way too focused on what people think of them, and you can't be because you're up against it. You know, this whole idea that if you're strong and powerful, you're a bitch, whereas a guy is just aggressive and ambitious, is really true. And you can't change that from being the perception, so you have to not care."

I couldn't agree more with Susie. I think women do care way too much about what people think of them. Particularly mothers. And I'm the worst offender. I'll bet I spend more time judging myself as a mom than I do sleeping. Former White House director of communications for President George W. Bush, political analyst, novelist, mother, and my friend Nicolle Wallace put it more cogently than I could. "Mothering isn't more important than fathering, but it's a standard by which we're measured. Mothering always makes us more vulnerable in how we're seen as women," she said in a conversation for this book. "I don't want to say 'judged,' but we are, mostly by ourselves."

No kidding. Many of us worry a great deal about our work lives eclipsing our family lives, and we buckle under the weight of our guilt. We are distracted by and worried about what people think. ("She's such a selfish, neglectful mother—she's away from her kids all week, and she still wants time to do her yoga classes!") We are worried about what we are doing and what we are supposed to be doing. (I should be picking my daughter up from track practice instead of writing this book.) Our visions of what our families look like and feel like—and the image we had for ourselves growing up and the path that we've actually taken—don't match in our own minds. The soft, embracing landing we thought we would find at home—the happy kids, the proud husband, the family rituals and adventures—is glaring at us when we enter the TV room after a long day at work. Your daughter is too busy snapchatting to say "Hi" and hang out for a little while. Your husband is already engrossed in his favorite show. We're afraid they resent us and think we take all the air out of the room; that because we spend so much time away at the office, we don't belong there. We have chosen against them.

Then again, maybe there is good reason to be worried that our career track has paved over our personal lives, that we've focused so intently on grooming and working our professional brand that our inner personal life is slowly withering from starvation. How do you know? What about the relationships that are sacrificed or take serious hits because of our career, our drive, the sheer hours on the job?

Be honest. Are your connections to your partner and your children suffering? What about doing the things that are important to your heart, mind, and spirit? Volunteering regularly at a women's shelter. Attending church, temple, mosque—whatever your place of worship—and being a vital part of that community. Launching a business or organization that you've always had a passion for. Drawing, painting, singing, sculpting, playing music. Even attending to your physical and mental health by exercising. There are activities that nurture us on many levels, that can sustain us through a demanding and stressful work life, and these can simply fall by the wayside. When we allow that to happen, we dismiss our inner value.

We don't really talk about it, but we have to. Now that we, as women, are working, succeeding, thriving, starting to negotiate for equal pay, and ascending into the upper ranks of leadership, I think we're confronting this issue head on. Remember the awkward moment at the White House Summit when I asked, "Any unexpected *personal strain* from that?" All the women on that panel knew what I was asking about: What happens to our inner lives as we achieve professional success? And no one wanted to answer the question. It's the part we won't discuss. And it's also the easiest part to lose when you're working like crazy. Most importantly, we will never fix this damaging cycle. But it should be fixable. After all, men seem to have this down.

A REALLY STRONG COMPASS

Sometimes we have to go back to the narrative of our own lives to remember who we are at our core, what our inner value is. I find that it helps to recall an early mentor who taught us something that shaped our perspective. I think about my own mother, for example. She, like me, was a late bloomer in finding herself in her career, and when she did, she positively blossomed. Unlike me, however, she has never been a people-pleaser. My mother has always been unapologetically herself. She steadfastly went her own way when my father was serving as national security advisor in President Jimmy Carter's White House. She preferred to do large-scale pruning (including felling trees) on our property and mucking around with our family's menagerie of farm animals than to attend the luncheons and soirees of Washington socialites. Whenever I start to overapologize, I think of my mother. That reminds me to tune into one of the chief prongs of my inner value—to advocate for myself and do what I think is right.

Dr. Judith Rodin had a wonderful story to share about how she came by her guiding star when I caught up with her after our meeting at the White House panel—she was much more willing to talk about the conflict between her career and personal life during a tête-à-tête than she was in front of an audience. "I had great advice from one of my elementary school teachers, and this is actually part of a rather embarrassing story. I was riding, and this shows my age, a trolley car in Philadelphia with my mother on a Saturday, and I was telling her that I was the teacher's pet and going on and on and mentioning my teacher by name and so forth," she laughed. "Well, on Monday I went to school and my teacher called me in and said, 'My mother was sitting in front of you and your mother on Saturday on the trolley car, and I wanted to tell you something that I hope you'll take throughout your life. I love you, I do, and I think you are wonderful. I love all my students. But the important thing is not whether or not I love you, but for the rest of your life, the key to success is to be your own most loyal fan and your own strongest critic. If you can rely on yourself to be both, you will surely succeed.' And I have never forgotten that. She took me away from always having to please others as a marker. I think part of my success was that I wasn't only focused on that, and it gave me a much truer North Star."

What a gift it is to learn early on how vital it is to avoid people-pleasing. Judith's wisdom itself is a gift—her deep knowledge of her worth as well as her limitations. As she spoke I could feel her radiating that kind of confidence. If you're looking for a role model, consider Judith. She speaks her mind, whether she's involved in a personal discussion or a boardroom meeting. There is no sense that there are two of her, the way I feel there is "work Mika" and "home Mika." You don't have the feeling that her professional value and inner value are at odds with each other; instead, they're blended.

To that point Judith went on to talk about how important it had been to her to develop her personal goals before she launched her career—to cleave to it throughout her brave albeit rocky path. "I think the one thing that worked most effectively was that I had a really strong compass, that I wanted to accomplish something. I wanted to make a difference in the world, and I felt that really early on," she said in her signature tone of absolute authority combined with compassionate wisdom. "I really felt that I wasn't going to be willing to give up, to not take the obstacles in my stride, and I knew it wasn't going to be easy."

No, it isn't easy. Over the years my observation has been that, as working women, we often feel massively guilty about not being with our families because we're working like crazy. So when we do manage to find some precious time just for ourselves, we don't take time to discover what—besides our families and our jobs—really motivates us, gives our hearts and souls a fire that burns with mission and meaning. It's as though we're not entitled to that part of our inner value, the part that belongs to us alone, as women, not only as mothers and wives. To develop it would be to neglect another, more important, part of our lives—like our families. Or so we tell ourselves at our own peril.

We have to stop doing this. (And in the upcoming chapters you'll read how Judith and many other amazing, powerful women have avoided this pitfall.) There is a massive divide between our professional worth and our personal goals. It has to be bridged if we are going to make it in life with any sense of purpose and heart. We will not be happy and we will not be truly successful until the two aspects of our lives are blended.

THAT INCLUDES LOTS OF OTHER PEOPLE

I have spoken to many women who have made it to the top of their game. Many of them have not made it without some personal failures along the way. There are strained marriages or divorces. There are children who miss their mother, are angry at the relentlessness of her career, and take it out on her when she's at home. There are passions that have been put on hold or extinguished. There is loneliness. But these women don't want to talk about it publicly; it's too private, too negative—too painful. Maybe they'll talk about it behind closed doors. They might discuss it with their closest friends. But that which we call the "work-family balance" is far, far from balanced—in fact, it's out of control.

And let's be honest: that is, *if* they've been able to nurture those relationships with their close friends between negotiating work and family time. More often than not, we're too busy to nurture friendships, a core feature of—in fact, studies have shown that friendships and community are essential to—our inner value.

Honestly, much of the time we're going it alone. It reminds me of something my mother said to me just this past summer when we were talking about the difficulties inherent in blending our professional and inner lives in a way that leaves us energized as well as peaceful. She put it so succinctly: "I think women have less chance than men to find their bliss."

One major part of our inner value that suffers is our commitment to our friends, our support network. In my experience it is your friendships—and maybe even more importantly, the sense that you have a strong community behind you and your family—that are often the most vulnerable links in keeping you grounded as a person. You work and work and work. And when you don't work, you want to be with your family every waking minute—or feel you should because your career has eclipsed your time with them. Moreover, you believe that all those waking minutes should be warm, happy, and close, spent doing fun, family things. When is there time to have coffee with a woman you've met and would really like to get to know better as possible friend material? The answer is that there isn't. You're too busy even to have long catch-up calls with old friends. You might not have spoken to them for close to a year. You assume they'll be there when you need them. But will they? And why should they be? I mean, I've developed friendships through business relationships. But to stop and have a new friendship outside of work? Honestly, there's no time.

When I was in labor with my second child and needed a backup ride to the hospital in case Jim hadn't come back from being out of town for work, I had to ask a woman I barely knew if she wouldn't mind driving me. Even then she agreed mostly because she was a longtime colleague of my husband's. And let's face it: because I'm working so much, I don't have a major sense of community in the town where I live; there isn't anyone there I could call on as a real friend.

I have some friendly acquaintances—mainly stay-at-home moms who used to think I wasn't so great for working when my kids were little, but who have been encouraging about my work now that we're sending our children off to college. But some of my encounters with the parents in town have been difficult because they've mainly revolved around our kids getting into trouble together. And because no one knew me, I became known as the crazy mom who went nuts on the parents in whose houses there was unsupervised drinking. Not the greatest way to meet your neighbors!

I am working on this now. I am calling it my personal PR effort in town. One mom and I recently had a good laugh about this. I used to know her only as "Lily's mom." Now she's Betsy Grass of Tommy Hilfiger. I discovered that we have a lot in common. We may even have dinner together with our girls!

In terms of close friends, I have one from growing up. I love her to death. But her story is so different from mine: she quit work after her first child, and she's been miserable. She openly talks about how her professional value and her inner worth plummeted. She has a business degree, had a great career. She's been out of the work force ten years. She's totally hirable, but she's going to have to take a big step back. I am coaching her, and she is always there for me. She doesn't live anywhere close to where I do, but even if she did, I'm not sure we'd actually see each other as often as I would want to. Again there just isn't the time. And if you haven't invested enough in your own personal life to make time to nurture and affirm those close friendships, they can easily fade away—like a language that you used speak fluently but haven't practiced for years. You can stumble your way through it, but you just don't know it like you used to. I thank God for the few friends who have held on to me and the few I have made at work.

But, according to Judith, we must maintain our friendships, our support systems. They are critical to working women's success, both as human beings growing our inner value and as professionals growing our professional value. Without friendships we can become isolated, lonely, humorless, and even depressed. "I think that you want to enrich not only your own relationships, but you need to enrich other relationships as well, whether that is in your work life or friendships. I think that when women are on that career track and working so hard, they do feel guilty at the time they're not spending at home—and are *made* to feel guilty—that what they give up even more are really good friendships and really good relationships and good supports. I think that actually worsens the tension at home, and has the potential to make you less successful at work," she pointed out. "So I think when you talk about balancing, I think balancing not only work and family life but balancing toward a more fulfilled life that includes lots of other people. And encouraging your spouse to have friends . . . because if you only focus on what the other is or isn't doing for you, the tension worsens."

Talking with Judith and reflecting on that anemic part of my life, I realized that I needed to make the time for friends. We all need to make the time—for our very health. In fact, when I looked into it, I found a major body of research that shows how important friendships are. For example, a study conducted by the Centre for Ageing Studies at Flinders University in South Australia followed nearly fifteen hundred older people for a decade. It found that those who had an ample, solid network of friends outlived those with the fewest by 22 percent. Close relationships with family, however, had no impact on longevity. Other studies have shown that having more friends reduces your chances of getting a cold, even though you're probably exposed to a greater number and variety of germs than those who have fewer social companions.

I also found research saying that people with a number of friends live longer after having major heart attacks, and they also have fewer cardiovascular and immune problems to begin with. Evidently friendship can even help women beat cancer. A study published by the journal *Cancer* showed that those women with advanced ovarian cancer who had reliable support from friends had much lower levels of a protein—known as interleukin 6, or IL-6—that appears in most aggressive types of cancer. Lower levels of IL-6 also improved the success of chemotherapy. But women with little support from friends had levels of IL-6 70 percent higher overall—and two and a half times higher in the area around the tumor. Amazing. Friendships can literally be lifesaving.

LOVE YOUR CHOICE

I am lucky to have forged friendships on the job with smart, ambitious, engaged women who teach me so much about the meaning of value. The amazing Arianna Huffington has become a good friend, as has the aforementioned designer of the Milly label, Michelle Smith, as well as presidential adviser Valerie Jarrett. Another awe-inspiring woman I've met over the course of my tenure as a broadcast journalist is Nicolle Wallace, who often joins us on *Morning Joe* in our panel discussions. Sometimes we are most closely put in touch with what matters most to us when we have hit bottom. No one, perhaps, understands this better than Nicolle.

Some years after her service at the White House, Nicolle went to work as senior adviser on the high-wire act that was the McCain-Palin campaign of 2008. At the outset of the campaign Sarah Palin had famously stumbled over herself. The shocking gaps in her knowledge of financial and political affairs were laid bare on national television, and her gaffes were constant. Then, however, she had gone on to enjoy popularity among voters leaning toward Tea Party affiliation—and she started to speak up in surprising and from-the-hip ways that had the ring of off-script vamping.

When the press started sniffing out the story, Nicolle was accused of anonymously leaking that Palin had "gone rogue," disobeying campaign managers' orders in order to advance her own career.

That was when Nicolle retired from politics. With the professional reputation that she had worked so incredibly hard to define and polish now tarnished by the worst kind of rumor mongering, she had to hang onto her sense of worth to get her through a dark and difficult time. But first she had to process the very political, very public firestorm she had walked through. A major part of finding her inner value was coming to terms with letting go of her professional value as it had been in that incarnation.

"To be a political campaign professional, to be accused of hurting the candidate, is a capital offense in politics. That's something I never would have done and something that crushed me to my core," she told me. "I spent twelve years sort of as a 'tip of the spear' position on campaigns and for politicians who were very well respected. I mean, I was twenty-five when I worked for Jeb Bush. When I went into the White House, I was twenty-eight years old. I had never made a mistake. I had never had a public misjudgment. I had never been suspected of doing anything other than my best for the politicians for whom I worked. But to work toward the end of my political campaign experience for someone who suspected me of doing what is really the gravest sin in politics was just professionally and personally disorienting and devastating. And in terms of my brand, you are unemployable in politics if people think you might be a person who reveals secrets of the campaign. You are unemployable," she repeated.

After the McCain-Palin campaign, Nicolle took personal inventory. She reflected on the brutality of politics and what it does to smart, committed, tenacious women, what it had done to her and, as she had witnessed, to the full spectrum of female politicians. Is it possible to maintain your integrity in politics? How do you keep control or let it go? How do you save your dignity when mud is relentlessly slung in your face?

Nicolle decided to explore these questions through writing fiction as a way to process all that she had endured and witnessed. "Instead of trying to rehabilitate my political brand, I thought that maybe it was just a sign or an opportunity to do something else. So that was when I got the idea for writing the novel. When I thought I could put it all into sort of a fictional place," she said. "I became obsessed with what happens to women in the meat grinder of politics. Obsessed. Not just because of my own experience, just because of Palin, but because that was the year of the Hillary Clinton primary where I felt—and maybe because it wasn't my political party—I felt like I was watching people root down the woman. And because I was neutral—I wasn't rooting for Obama, I wasn't rooting for Hillary—I really saw it that way. So that really inspired . . . I don't want to call it a creative process . . . it just made me want to sort of deal with all this stuff.

"I think after Palin I was either going to therapy or write three novels. I'm happy I decided to write three novels. I got to play with all this stuff—people being obsessed with what you wear, women warring with women. All these things that sort of became my life. I didn't want to talk about them in a tell-all way, but I did want to play with all those topics."

After the novel was published, Nicolle had her talent and inner value affirmed by women she met while traveling around the country, giving readings and making appearances. "When I went on book tour, all these women who were Democrats would come up to me and say, 'Oh my God, what happened to Charlotte [the name of Nicolle's first female president character] is what happened to Hillary," or they'd see themselves. So I really feel like—and your books deal with this too—women are so silent about something that we all see. And then when you start talking about it, heads nod. It's such a common experience, and it's not unique to politics or television. It's literally every workplace, and I think women struggle to form tribes and bands as easily and neatly as men do," she said. "The Palin experience, in the moment, was horrible, but professionally and personally nothing that came after it would have been possible without it. Nothing."

Wow. It's a powerful story (and this was the first of several of Nicolle's rebranding turning points, as you'll read in Chapter 9). Frankly I stand in admiration of how Nicolle was able to recognize her inner value during some of her most harrowing moments, to transform both her pain and wisdom into creating a fictional world that mirrored her own—and in the process launch a whole new brand as a novelist and TV commentator! But that's not all. During this period Nicolle and her husband also had a baby boy.

When she became a mom and a novelist, Nicolle made the decision to work from home, getting babysitting help on her four writing days out of the week. Being with her son and getting the full experience of motherhood for the first time are hugely important to Nicolle, and switching gears professionally and personally has allowed her to grow these aspects of herself. She almost feels, she says, that her life is "too good." "I think it's important to love your choice, realizing that men don't get to make it," she said. "There's no expectation that men *may* choose this or *may* choose that. No one asked my husband what *he* was going to do when the baby came. And getting to choose at all is an elite problem."

Does she feel like she has it all? Nicolle was circumspect. "The model for 'having it all' is the Sarah Jessica Parker character as the investment banker in *I Don't Know How She Does It*, and we see her sacrifices. For every woman who wishes she could put on a fabulous suit and a five-hundred-dollar pair of Manolo Blahniks and go to the office, there's a working mom walking away from the school bus with tears in her eyes because she never gets to see her kids," she said. For Nicolle, having it all always meant something different. "I think I always knew I wanted to put the brakes on when I had kids. Having it all never meant doing it all at the same time."

Nicolle Wallace is an example for all women. Her life is an incredible illustration of professional value overlapping with inner value, and I love how it frames the central question of this book—certainly of my life and quite possibly yours: How do you combine your professional and personal worth in your life? How can you bridge the two in ways that make you feel truly successful, as a whole, while still making a profit?

Answer number one: not perfectly.

CHAPTER FOUR

WORKING YOUR VALUE

Using Your Professional and Inner Value to Get What You Want

I know a woman in the print and broadcast news business, also an author, who was at the top of her game by the time she reached her early thirties. Throughout her twenties she'd written for the *Wall Street Journal* and the *Washington Post*, had a column in *Glamour*, was on the original team that launched Time Inc. on the web, and was a playwright. At twenty-seven she was senior editor at *US News & World Report*; at twenty-eight she was cohosting and cowriting a popular technology show for public television. At thirty she was married, and at thirty-one had her first child. When her daughter turned three months old—at the end of her maternity leave—she got a call from a bigwig producer recruiting her to be an anchor at a major cable news network.

It was a big job. Possibly *the* big job. But then she looked at her little cutie kicking her little legs and thought, *Can't do it.* She called back and demurred. She would, instead, freelance for magazines and newspapers, write a book or two. And she was fine with that decision. Sure, she would keep a hand in her field, but more importantly she really wanted to be a hands-on mom.

The woman is journalist Susan Gregory Thomas, author of *In Spite of Everything: A Memoir*, and my collaborator on this book. Now forty-six, her plan didn't go as expected. Susie, as her friends call her, is divorced from her daughters' father, remarried, and living with her family of five, all of whom somehow huddle into a two-bedroom apartment (the adults sleep on a couch in the living room, and the kids divvy up the bedrooms). She has elevated her professional value and expertise as an observer of generational differences—Baby Boomers, Generation X, and Millennials—and has also managed to get great book deals over the years. Still, she has spent the past seven years trying to keep her family afloat on a freelancer's and book author's earnings. And it has been far from easy.

Now does she wish she'd taken that job?

"I knew as soon as my daughter was born that I would have to divide myself into two people to keep my professional value growing at the kind of turbo rate at which it was careening along back then—and I just couldn't do it," she said to me. "I would have been miserable—eaten up with regret. So I'm still glad I made the decision I did. But life hasn't been easy financially. On the contrary, it is very, very scary. I have to run twice as fast to stay in the same place, and even so, there's been a lot of backsliding, particularly during the recession."

Our experiences are so different yet spookily parallel. Where I sacrificed a great deal of my inner value as a mother and wife to feed my growing professional value (and, along with it, getting my financial worth), Susie went exactly the opposite route as a TV journalist and author. I, on the one hand, had seized my "big job" moment with *Morning Joe*; I love my job, and I'm compensated well for it. But I am haunted by the time I've missed—and still do—with my family over the years. On the other hand, Susie had turned down the big TV morning show host offer to be with her children, and she is happy with her work. But she'd lost one marriage and a substantial income in spite of it anyway. We both have enjoyed major gains. And we both have suffered major losses.

So do I dare ask the question that's on my mind? Hell, yes: Who made the better decision? Or, phrased another way: Who is more successful in merging her inner and professional lives?

I was interested in a point Susie had made about how her work and home overlap. "Since I work from home, it's possible that my professional self and my mom self are 'integrated' to a greater degree than working mothers who have that clear line between office and home. My children are at school mostly when I'm working, but when you're a freelancer, the work clock never really stops. So my children see me working. And they have to deal with it. Because Mommy has to work," she explained.

"There have been times when I'm interviewing someone for a magazine story or book, and for scheduling reasons the interview has to happen at dinner time or just around bed-time. My kids start to squabble or laugh too loudly, and I have to say, 'Excuse me, could you pardon me for just a moment?' I'll mute the phone and bark at my kids if they don't zip it now, we're going to be living on the street starting tomorrow morning. They know I'm joking, but at the same time, they get that it's serious." Does she feel guilty that she has to shunt her kids to the side for work, at home, when family time is supposed to be happening? "Sometimes I do, if I'm really in crunch-down, deadline mode. But at the same time, all of us know that my work keeps the ecosystem in balance," she said. "What I mean is: *we're* like an ecosystem. I may be the domi-nant animal in it, but all its constituent critters and activities are vital to our habitat's health and functioning. All of us are constantly adapting to each of its changing needs."

The concept of the family as ecosystem really appeals to me as a model for working families. I know that I, for one, am grafted to the old idea that the home has to be a castle, a haven away from work, a family-time-only zone. But I run into a lot of problems because of it. That dictum puts a lot of pressure on working parents to transform into a completely different person at home—I would argue, particularly work-ing mothers. You go from being, for example, a hard-driving executive at work, where you can't talk about home life, to being an understanding and devoted mother and spouse, where you're not supposed to talk about work for more than five minutes after you first walk in through the door. You have to check a major cross-section of yourself at the door-way at work as well as at home. Your professional value and inner value are completely split. You can feel as if you're schizoid.

The way we all earn a living now—even if we're not working from home—means that work invariably enters home. And it shouldn't be seen as evil. Of course, workaholism is a different issue, but for most of us work is simply a vital part of life, of the ecosystem, and it should be seen that way. If you're at home and you have to spend half an hour answering an important e-mail or you have to check a text coming in from a different time zone—so what? If you come home and your professional personality is still going at full tilt, what's the problem? Why should it be so terrible that your partner and children see you in work mode? Kids often have a different persona with their friends and at school—in the public domain—from their persona at home. Isn't there an argument for working parents to be transparent so kids learn that it's natural to shift between different styles of interacting in the full spectrum of life circumstances? I find myself pretending to be Mommy at home and Mika Brzezinski at work. Do I have to hide them from each other? Can't the two overlap without me going into an awkward, guilty dance?

I look at Susie, and I see someone who passed up an opportunity to get paid her worth and, more, to invest in her professional value and secure her future. I see an exhausted woman who's always working twice as hard, as she herself says, to stay in the same place. But I also see a talented author who has gotten to write fantastic books that she's loved working on, as well as a mother who is completely comfortable and loving with her kids.

When I look at myself, I see a wife and mother whose relationships with her family seem hinged together by gum and paper clips or whatever spackle or surrogate I can grab at any given moment. But I also see that I am earning my professional value, growing my professional brand, and, through my work helping women to understand their worth, developing a discrete but vibrant part of my inner value. Neither one of us has balance in her life. Neither one of us can be said to "have it all."

The question is not about who made the better decision; instead, we should ask what we can do, as working women, to grow our value overall so that we can be as successful and fulfilled as possible. How can we take features of our needs and goals and deploy them in the marketplace and vice versa? Can we work our professional brand into our personal lives? How can we bridge the two in ways that make us feel truly successful as a whole? Ultimately we'll know we've been successful when our two declarative statements about our professional value and inner value are one. We'll be earning what we're worth. We'll accept our regrets, even if they linger. We'll define and exert our boundaries and limitations, even if they're pushed. We'll feel at peace both at work and at home.

But how is that going to happen?

VERY MUCH ME

We're not there yet. According to our Working Women Study Poll, although the majority of breadwinners in the United States, regardless of gender, agree with the statement that "it is possible to have it all," one in four (22 percent) female breadwinners and 13 percent of male breadwinners disagree with it. What does a statistic like that tell us?

I know what it tells me. I'll bet if you were a fly on the wall at their houses or over coffee with their friends, you'd get a much, much higher number. I mean, when you talk with working women and men on the ground, in ordinary conversation, do you ever, *ever* hear them gloat, "I'm having it all! My work life and personal life are in complete balance!" Are you kidding me? Statistics like the one our poll turned up say to me that this generation of successful working women and men—raised in and around the Feminist Movement—are putting on their game faces and striving for that nonexistent balance.

Maybe we shouldn't be surprised. This is the generation, after all, who spends as much time with their children as possible to make up, in part, for their own "home alone" childhoods. I don't blame them for wanting to believe they can have it all—that there are no consequences on the home front for pursuing their careers. To admit that there are holes in the system would be tantamount to admitting that, at least to some degree, they're repeating their own childhoods with their own children.

It doesn't feel emotionally acceptable to say this out loud, especially for women. We're the ones who are supposed to be making the feminist dream come true. We don't want to fall short. We don't want our kids to live through anything remotely like what we did. After all, 40 percent of children under eighteen growing up in the 1980s were latchkey kids, wearing the keys to their homes around their necks so they could let themselves in after school because no parent was at home—often, it was their single, working moms who were absent. We don't want our kids to feel abandoned because of our careers, the way we did, for better or for worse. Who wants to admit this? Only some working women are willing to say "having it all" isn't going as planned—to the not-insignificant tune of one in four.

Still, to admit that there are problems with that premise takes real guts. In a period of US history fast becoming the Age of Women, I think it takes a lot of courage to say publicly: "This isn't working for me." Interestingly, however, our poll did ferret out a lot of "this isn't working for me" responses by rephrasing the question. When they were asked whether or not they enjoy being the breadwinner, fully two-thirds (63 percent) of female breadwinners said they don't enjoy being the primary earner or that it is a "mixed bag," compared with four in ten male breadwinners (38 percent). Not only that, but female sole earners are twice as likely as male sole earners to say that their role as the breadwinner in the relationship is a "mixed bag" or one they do not enjoy (79 percent versus 39 percent). My guess? Women are, as Susie said, working twice as hard to stay in the same place.

That does not sound like "having it all" to me. Women cannot possibly have it all if our professional values and inner values aren't closely allied *and* aligned.

For some of us those values do coexist and intertwine—even if it has taken a lifetime so far to get there. Me, for example. I spent decades trying to be what I thought people wanted me to be at work and then having nothing left when

I got home. I had no sense of my professional or inner worth. After years of trial and lots and lots of error, now what I do for a living is very much *me*. I am myself on *Morning Joe*. I am very much myself in passing along the message to women of knowing and growing your value. It's in doing this work that my values converge. Helping women talk and learn about this is something that I do not just for the sake of expanding business, but because it is a natural facet of who I am. Writing books about women's value and helping them get what they're worth. Hosting live conferences, where real women join me onstage to struggle through articulating their value. My professional bona fides as a straight-dealing (and kind of funny, or so I've been told) news talk-show host overlaps with the part of my inner calling that cares about working women, empathizes with them, and wants deeply for them to flourish. In this area of my life I can honestly say that I feel successful.

The discovery along the way of who the inner and outer Mika are and encouraging them to be friends is not a chore for me—it's what I want to do. It's my most favorite thing to do. Even better, my girls are getting involved with this movement I'm trying to build, and I am getting involved with their lives in a very real way. As they wander into adulthood, I am finding that they think their mom is useful, possibly even cool. This feels really good. It is helping them question early on what the substance of their inner value and burgeoning professional value really are. And I finally feel like I'm doing something for my girls. It is all coming together for us as a family.

YOU SHOULD GO FOR THAT

I had an amazing conversation about integrating personality and professional value with Cindi Leive, editor-in-chief of *Glamour*. "I remember when, pretty early on in my career, I was in some ways a very ambitious young editor, but I wasn't really thinking about the job I wanted to end up with. I just always knew that whatever job I had, I wanted to get to the next one. But I didn't necessarily think of myself as someone who would become an editor-in-chief. . . . I was sort of senior-editor level, and most of the editors-in-chief were quite a bit older than me," she said. "There was an editor-in-chief position open at a magazine at a competitive company, and I had heard about it—I had engaged in gossip about who would get that job. It literally never once occurred to me that I should raise my hand for that job. I remember a friend of mine e-mailing me, a former colleague, someone who had been a mentor to me, saying, 'Hey, I don't know if you know that the editor-in-chief position at such-and-such place is open. You should go for that. You would be great.'

"And it was like this light bulb went off in my mind. . . . It literally had not occurred to me that even though I knew about that job, thought it was a great job for someone else, but that that someone else could be me. It seemed so obvious afterward that *yes*, I was a completely legitimate candidate for that job," she said with enthusiasm. "I didn't get it. It probably was a little bit of a stretch for me to apply for it. But not a big stretch. A teeny stretch of the sort we should all be doing every day. And it's like that classic thing they say about how women have to be tapped on the shoulder and asked seven times before they run for office, before they do it. It was not until someone literally, virtually, tapped me on the shoulder that I thought, 'Oh, duh . . . why not me?'"

Now, as editor-in-chief of one of the most successful women's magazines of all time, Cindi reflects on how one aspect of her personality that she's always had has helped her in her career: native cheerfulness. "A part of succeeding in any kind of top job is being confident, being fairly optimistic," she said. "[You can't] run a successful business if you are pessimistic or cynical, because there are going to be things that go wrong every day. You have to believe that you are going to find a way out of them, that your team is going to find a way out of them."

IN A ROOM WITH REALLY SMART PEOPLE

Cindi went on to deploy that same confidence and sunny personality in order to learn how to network. This process contributed to her vision as a leader and confidence as a woman. "I think one thing that women don't do enough of to grow their value . . . [is the] relationship-growing that . . . happens outside of the workplace and in trade organizations. I think it took me a while in my career to know that being on boards, plugging myself into other great things that were going on in the industry, being out and about, just building great relationships with people both in my industry and women and men I might want to cover in the magazine," she explained. "All of that was good for my career and good for whoever was employing me. I think there's a certain amount of kind of guilt that some women feel when you sneak off to network . . . and also women feel they're being disloyal to their employer if they do that," she pointed out. "But if you are growing your value that way, you are much more valuable to whoever signs your paycheck. You are a more plugged-in employee; you're more savvy. You know what's going on in your industry. You can explain things to people that you work with."

This totally spoke to me. When people talk about "the boys' club" in any industry, we all know that they're talking about men networking outside the office walls to make connections, to get ahead in their careers. And what do women do? As Cindi said, they feel *guilty* because if they network with a competitor, they think that could conceivably be seen as being a disloyal employee. Are we kidding? It reminds me of my daughters'—and my own—junior high girls' tacit social regulations. If you were friends with Amanda and her friends, for example, you could not sit next to Liza and her friends at lunch. Ever. Even if it were to find out where Liza had bought that cute sweater no one else could find at the mall. Translated into the world of professional networking as working women, as Cindi pointed out, even if we're collecting valuable information on behalf of our organization, we feel as though eyes are on us in the lunchroom—that someone's going to get back to Amanda and tell her what a two-faced you-know-what you are.

To grow our professional value we absolutely have to stop thinking this way. We need to graduate from junior high.

Because just as alliances and group formations shift quickly and dramatically with girls of that age, so do companies, trends, and the industry stars of the moment. As Cindi pointed out, it is up to us to know that, although we owe allegiance to the company for which we're working now, ultimately we're always brand-building, gathering knowledge, and making connections that keep us current and essential to our employers—and on the job market. It positions us as active, ambitious players in our fields; that is, we are not only women who have a job at a certain company but also who have our own particular professional brands that are becoming well known and, if we work it right, respected by and attractive to the industry at large.

Cindi went on, ruminating on how networking had not only improved her inner value by making deep and lasting personal connections but had also helped her strategically steer *Glamour* during a time of flux. "I spent a couple years as president of American Society of Magazine Editors, and I feel like not only did I make relationships with some of the best brains in the media business and longtime friendships and relationships that have lasted over a decade, but I intentionally did it at a moment when the magazine industry was changing. It was right at the advent of digital, and everybody in our business was kind of looking around and—excuse me—going, 'Holy shit! Is the Titanic going down, or are we all going to become speedboats and it's going to be okay?'" she recalled. "And being able to place myself in a boardroom with really smart people once a month for an hour and hear how they were coping and what they thought . . . really broadened my horizons and made me a much better editor-in-chief, a much better member of the media community, and gave me a ton of ideas I wouldn't have had otherwise. I think it's easy to suffer from that career myopia where you're just head-down at your desk doing whatever gets handed to you that day."

THE DIFFERENCE BETWEEN BRAVE AND COCKY

Cindi nailed it completely. I cannot stress it enough: if we are going to grow our professional and inner worth, meeting people who either are or could one day be valuable associates, potential future colleagues or bosses, connectors, collaborators—and also personal friends—is simply essential. I see every moment out of my house (except when I'm on vacation) as a networking opportunity because I almost always get something out of every encounter. There should be nothing wrong about that.

But there is one thing I don't do anymore. As I stated earlier, I do not do people-pleasing.

Networking is not about trying to get everyone to like you. It's not about making close friends. I've said it before and I'll say it again now: people-pleasing is poison. It is enemy number one for women who want to grow personally and professionally. It actually saps your value. If you are trying to be all things to all people, you will not leave a solid impression on anyone nor will you make any genuinely useful contacts. If you keep it up, eventually you will be seen as a sycophant, someone not to be trusted or taken seriously. People can usually sense an acting job, and that will make them uneasy and unsure about what your motives and intentions are. At best you won't be seen as a serious person; at worst you'll be looked on as vaguely devious and untrustworthy. In addition, people-pleasing will run you ragged. Networking, however, is seeing that there may be a useful connection between two people. It is either there or it is not.

Even more importantly, if you are playing to the crowd, you may be giving them what you think they want, but you will not be getting what you want or need. To network effectively you must communicate who you are and what you have to offer. This is not to say it's permissible to be rude; it is never permissible to be rude. But it is permissible—in fact, it's *advisable*—to be powerful, open, fearless.

For example, at a women's awards event I met a woman named Nadja Bellan-White, an executive at the advertising firm Ogilvy & Mather. We got to chatting, and it turned out that she was in the running to head up Ogilvy Africa. "When the CEO of North America warned me I was about to get called into the offices soon, and my first reaction was, 'Oh boy . . . what client situation has occurred now?'" she said.

I moaned in complete sympathy. So typical of us women, isn't it? We're such people-pleasers that if the higher-ups want to talk to us, we expect that we're in trouble rather than assume that good news is coming our way. I gave her my one-minute lecture on the importance of knowing her value, told her about my experience negotiating my salary at *Morning Joe*, and encouraged her to pick up my book before she went into further discussions with the muckety-mucks so she could make sure to get her money's worth while considering the offer. She read the book that night.

Next thing you know Nadja's e-mailing and calling me to tell me about how she'd negotiated the Ogilvy Africa CEO position. "I went from thinking 'why me?' to 'why *not* me'? I stopped apologizing. Still, I was afraid. Can I *do* this? Will I have the resources to get the job done?" she told me. "[Your] book was about succeeding, so I started thinking, 'What would happen if *I* succeeded?' I think that kind of bravery is frowned on in women. But there's a difference between being brave and cocky, and I think that's a line that men don't seem to negotiate as finely as professional women."

To that end Nadja told me that not only had she worked her professional value to negotiate an appropriate compensation package, but she had also protected her inner value by speaking up about what she would need for her family to make such a major move for the job. "I became brave enough to speak up about things like, would my kids and husband be okay? If you're a working mother, these are the things you talk about. Will my family adjust? Is this too much for them? Should I just not do it? My son is twelve and a half, has a promising career in baseball," she said. "I wrote up three columns of what I felt we needed. Management, for example, wanted us to visit the kids' school virtually. And I negotiated for a trip for my kids to visit their school in person. By the third round I felt like I was getting there in terms of my confidence and competence level." In the end Nadja got almost all of her requirements met, and she accepted the position as CEO of Ogilvy Africa. She was brimming with excitement when she told me the news. "Your book inspired me to ask for what I deserved!" she exclaimed. I explained that this was great, but Nadja ultimately got the job due to her competence, drive, and ability to communicate effectively for herself.

Think about what a powerful experience of networking this is. By making a simple connection at an event, Nadja and I exchanged experiences, and I encouraged her to learn from mine. She ended up reading my book and using the advice to reach an incredible deal as CEO of Ogilvy Africa. I, in turn, got to hear and learn from her amazing story. She then recommended my book to her network of contacts here and around the world. (I think she is starting a movement in Africa!) Now we both have a powerful personal and professional contact in each other. And I firmly believe that our networking connection worked because she was frank about questioning her professional and inner value, and I was clear in communicating mine to help inspire her to take the next step. To her point, if either one of us had been cocky rather than brave, our meeting might not have been so fruitful.

AN OPPORTUNITY TO BE A ROLE MODEL

Networking with other professional women isn't always just a chance opportunity. At some companies women's networking is stitched into the corporate fabric. At General Electric, for example, the in-house "Women's Network," founded in the mid-1990s by pioneering female executives, not only provides a safe place for women in the company to discuss issues they face at work but also serves as a talent pool for recruiting and advancing women to different positions across the entire corporation. In so doing women who are part of the Women's

Network are able to grow professionally as corporate employees interested in advancing at GE as well as personally as
working women and mothers in what was a traditional male
workplace until the group took off.

Denice Biocca, a senior human resources leader within GE
Oil and Gas, owes the growth of her career to GE's Women's
Network, having been an active member since its start. "I started
in a manufacturing facility providing human resources support
to hourly employees. . . . I was the number two in the plant of
two [HR reps]. . . . My manager who hired me into the company was pretty instrumental in assimilating me into the
company, and shortly after, my manager moved on to another
position, and her position was open. At the time I had been
about a year at the company, and I didn't know how to advance
my career at GE. So naturally the job I thought I wanted to do
next was her job," she said during a phone interview.

"So she left me in the role, and I'm helping to interview
candidates to replace her and coordinating visits for my
potential new boss coming in, and at the same time, I raised
my hand and said that I would like to be considered for that
job. And I was told, 'You really don't have the experience that
we're looking for.' As things go, it takes some time before you
fill a job, and while I was acting [HR leader], our general manager, who was really one of the foremothers of our GE Wom-
en's Network, was my first sponsor. She stepped up and said,
'Hey, I've interviewed these other candidates that you've sent
down here for me to take a look at, but I think Denice is
stronger than any of them I've seen. I know we've said she's
not ready for this level of job yet, but . . . I am an advocate for

her, and I want her in the job.' That was my first experience in GE of having a very personal sponsor who stepped up and said they wanted me for the job even though arguably I didn't have all the experience. . . . I had met her as she was coming into the job, we were starting the Women's Network at the time, and she had asked me as the HR person on the site for my ideas and opinions on some of the ideas she had been bouncing around."

Having experienced firsthand the power of the Women's Network to provide connections, Denice became further involved with the group. In its nascent stages the Network's goal was to help women at the company learn how to present themselves and their accomplishments so they could better put themselves in line for advancement. This was a way for women who had learned the ropes to help those with less experience to polish, promote, and grow their value at the company.

Denice said that as the Women's Network grew, so did its reach and influence throughout GE. As she herself moved up in her career at GE over the next sixteen years, she came to regard it as a forum from which she could, as an HR executive, not just look for talent but also use as a test for innovating and structuring new woman-friendly work policies. In addition, she could network there to keep smart, hard-working women at the company—and to keep them happy.

"By the late 1990s we were trying to retain talent, and we wanted to use the Women's Network as a tool. We hosted round-table discussions with women, and I led many of those discussions. We asked three questions: 'One, what brought you to GE? Two, what's going on that makes you get up and continue to come back to GE? And three, when you think about leaving GE, what's happening?' It was an unbelievably simple initiative. You could go to a safe space with eight to ten other women and you could talk about what was going on," she said. Everyone from junior-level women to those who had been at the company for years felt comfortable opening up, Denice said.

Before long the top-line issues for women on the job began to surface. "The themes that were coming out were: 'I'm working in isolation'; 'I'm the only woman in my engineering group, and I want to do more, and I keep getting told to do my job. How do I show my manager that I can do more when I'm working on a team that's very structured?'; and 'I need some flexibility because I have a brand-new baby and I'm afraid to ask for permission to leave early.'"

Important personnel and corporate culture changes came out of the frank conversations Denice and others in the Women's Network facilitated, many of which are embedded in the company today. "One [of them] is having a buddy system where you can call on someone else and say, 'Have you ever had this situation before, and what did you do?'" she said. "At a broader level, as an HR professional, I was able to draw on some of those themes and shape change for work flexibility, intervening on a personal level or being a part of changing policies. The biggest [policy changes] are around how we do flexible work arrangements . . . now we're working on the culture, so flexibility is inferred."

Speaking of flexible work schedules, a few years after the Women's Network launched, a subdivision grew out of it. The Network launched a small group peer mentoring program called myConnections. From that group's outset grew a GE Working Moms' Group that attracted more than a hundred women in their twenties, thirties, and forties. The group raised issues such as onsite day care, breastfeeding rooms, and flextime. Today, Denice said, thanks to the popular and influential group, she can leave early twice a week to take her son, who has developmental needs, to therapy without special dispensation.

Denice said, "Those of us in senior positions have an important opportunity to role model flexibility"—streamlining their professional value as executives at the corporation with their inner value as mothers who needed flexibility to take care of their children. The opportunity soon presented itself. She was in a big conference room meeting at the end of the work day, she said, when the presentation was running long. Denice knew that it wasn't just her who was getting worried she'd be late to pick up her children, but that there were also several other women junior to her in the meeting who were looking nervous about the same thing—something she knew because those women were part of the Working Moms Group.

Realizing that she was the senior executive in the room, Denice decided to take action and show the other mothers as well as everyone in the meeting that senior leadership considered it important to honor employees' family and personal commitments—that this was definitely part of GE's work culture. "I stood up and said, 'We're going to wrap this up because we're already twenty minutes over, and I know that they are at least three of us in this room who have to go pick up our kids,'" she said. What a powerful example of "crossing the streams" of professional and personal power!

Denice's path to leadership and GE's senior management's willingness to support the Women's Network and families' needs is very impressive. Hearing about how this cooperative corporate effort encourages simultaneously the growth of women's professional value and their inner value gave me great hope for the possibility of integrated life at work. Communication was the key to making it all work.

MAXIMIZING ENERGY WHILE MANAGING STRESS

Another corporate effort that I really admire is Johnson & Johnson's Human Performance Institute, a team based in Orlando that hosts programs to help corporate leaders and their organizations boost their vigor and perform at their peaks. The Institute's flagship workshop, the Corporate Athlete, is a two-and-a-half-day training program focused on expanding and managing individual energy capacity. The course helps people become more productive under pressure as well as sustain high performance both at work and at home. It's literally designed to help hard-driving people harness their energy and convert it into personal and professional value. With more than thirty years of experience, the Institute's team is staffed with trained coaches, physiologists, and nutritionists who have trained and learned the performance secrets of people in high-stress fields, from Olympic medalists, elite professional athletes, CEOs, hostage rescue teams, and military Special Forces. And Johnson & Johnson employees. Specifically, women.

I had the chance to talk with Alex Gorsky, the CEO of Johnson & Johnson, and I asked him about why the company made attending workshops at the Institute such a top priority for women. "I believe that human energy is the currency of high performance, and training to expand and manage energy is the key to being extraordinary in work and life. And I've heard a lot, particularly with our female leaders, about this whole issue of, 'How do I manage my energy across the multiple demands that I have? How am I really showing up and being there for my family? How do I show up at work, with the right amount [of energy]?'" he explained. "It's no small feat. I think [training at the Human Performance Institute] gives you a framework and lots of practical tools and ways of managing the different components and parts of your life. We've put thirty-eight thousand people through HPI—including most of our senior leaders. We use it actually as a team-building exercise. It's one of the most impactful things [we do]."

Alex went on to talk about how important he and Johnson & Johnson believe it is for women in particular to take care of themselves. "I think it's particularly important to women. These jobs are tough. They're demanding. Last year's performance becomes this year's baseline. You suffer [from] traveling . . . it's tough to be connected. And what you don't want to do is go twenty-five, thirty years, and you've given completely of yourself to your career, and you haven't taken the time to do what can be relatively simple things to take care of yourself. And then you have some untoward health event. We know so many of the issues that we face from a disease burden or a health issue are modulated by how we deal with stress, how we deal with eating, how we deal with exercise," he continued. "So you've given all this up, you've compromised all this, and you have some untoward health event, and your family never gets all that benefit. That's a terrible place to be. And so we don't only want to be the largest health care company, we want to be the healthiest and to thrive at work and home. That means you have to take care of yourself."

I also wanted to know how the company responds to women when they need flextime because of family reasons but they still want to stay in the game. I told Alex about a conversation with the CEO of a global company who wanted some advice from my Know Your Value concept. He believed that women didn't feel they could come in and say, "Listen, obviously you want to keep me here, you want me to stay here, but I'm going to need to make some changes because my child has special needs, and I've got to focus on that. I've got to scale back, but I want to stay on track." Is there, I asked Alex, a reticence on the part of women who are in a management position, who are on a track for growth, to feel confident enough to say, "I need something"? He had some interesting answers.

"We do that routinely. In fact, as we go through succession planning, it is a very common event, particularly if you have a woman in her midthirties who is just about to become a director, and she's going to be having her second or third child, and she needs to do the infamous: 'I don't want to get off the exit ramp, but I do need to do a stay-in-place, have a flexible work schedule for the next eighteen or twenty-four months,' or, 'I'm not able to relocate during this period of time,' or, 'I may need to have this kind of flex schedule or work-share schedule but then come back on,'" he responded. "Now, I think it's fair to [say that] the caveat [is that we] look particularly at people who are high performers, who we see with high potential, [and then] I think that's one of the most critical inflection points we see in women's careers, is helping them through these critical times.

"And you've got to be able to look around and see that other women have done it, survived, and actually thrived. I think [it is important] when there are examples of that— where there are successful women in the organization who have done that," Alex continued. "I think you also have to be explicit about the programs and tools and what are the areas we are going to be willing to flex when it comes to geography, when it comes to work hours, when it comes to travel schedules, to home office. This is one thing where one size doesn't fit all. You've got to have multiple tools, and you've got to be flexible because every situation is going to be a little bit different."

I think that Johnson & Johnson's corporate initiative to help female leaders balance their work and home lives is amazing. And in fact, their message resonated with me so much that Johnson & Johnson is a presenting sponsor in the

Know Your Value national tour with NBC, helping women ten times more than we were able to in Hartford. Contestants from all over the country will have a chance to learn from experts at Johnson & Johnson's Human Performance Institute in Orlando, giving these women the opportunity to transform their lives and then sharing those stories on *Morning Joe* and on our MSNBC website.

CHAPTER FIVE

WOMEN BREADWINNERS-IN-CHIEF AT HOME

When Professional Life Meets Intimate Relationships

When I first started thinking about the idea for this book, I knew that I would have to write this chapter. I was scared then; I'm scared now. I know that there is a large delegation of successful, professional women who would probably prefer to talk about their adventures in mammography rather than to wade into the mucky territory of how their work life has impacted their marriages or partnerships—and how their mates have affected their careers. I completely get it. It's uncomfortable. It's fragile. It's *personal*. I mean, our families are supposed to be perfect, right? Isn't that the one true definition of a happy woman? Isn't it all supposed to look and feel so easy for all of us? In truth, none of our families are perfect, and I know that if I can't talk about my own struggles and share my conversations with successful working women about theirs, then I can't honestly talk about knowing and growing your value.

Simply put, I'd be a fraud. For me to say that I have found the path to true success in life by sticking to some map that other women and I had discovered would be nonsense. There is no map. No one knows *the* route. Don't believe people who say that there is one. What I, countless other professional women, and you *do* have is our experience and our reflections. Those are priceless, and it's important for us to share them with each other. Eventually they may all combine to create a map, illustrating a number of routes that will get you to where you want to be: a place of true success where your personal and professional selves gracefully overlap each other.

But what the data shows is that we're not there yet. Women breadwinners are growing in epic numbers, certainly. According to a 2013 Pew Research Center analysis of data from the US Census Bureau, an unprecedented 40 percent of all American households with children under the age of eighteen are supported by mothers who are either the sole or primary source of income for the family. They're not having an easy time of it (and I'll get into our poll results on that momentarily). But I also want to share with you what my experience has shown me and what my conversations with successful working women have shown. And that is: as our professional lives and professional values grow, the dynamics—even the language—of our closest connections with our most intimate companions are reshaped, upset, and transformed. Sometimes drastically. If we began our relationships early as young adults, we are, in many ways, no longer the same women we were when we first met our partners.

For some couples these changes are positive. For them the shifts in positions, outlooks, and responsibilities have allowed both partners to occupy roles in their relationship that are unique and perfectly suited to them. But there are many of us who have been blindsided by the unexpected emotional fees and taxes attached (often, in vague, passive-aggressive print) to our rise in professional success.

That's another reason why this chapter scares me. I'm going to put myself out there, and I'm going to share discussions with other women who put themselves out there too. We have to do it. This tension in relationships is becoming a cultural issue. We're living in a unique time in American history. Not only do most women work now, but they're also surpassing men in education and salaries. In particular I think women who make more than their husbands have unexpected challenges, and data exists that shows that, even in our postfeminist, egalitarian democracy. So if we don't start a national conversation about this now, it's going to hurt our children later.

AND THEN I GOT A RAISE

My husband, Jim, and I have always had a marriage of equals. We'd both grown up as children when the Women's Movement and ERA were in full swing. We worked in the same field. Jim and I have always been in the television news business. In fact, as I mentioned earlier, that's how we met, in our twenties, working at a local news station in Hartford, Connecticut, where Jim was hands down the most thorough, smart, analytical investigative reporter in the pack (and still is).

From the beginning of our relationship and marriage Jim and I were always working breakneck deadlines, often passing each other like speedboats in the night. We understood and respected each other's work ethic. We supported each other. We still support each other. But over the past several years my professional presence and persona have gotten to be increasingly public. I started making more money than he did. And then I got a raise. A big raise.

I didn't tell him about it for two months.

Why? Why wasn't I sharing this amazing news—the news of my professional lifetime—with Jim immediately? Why weren't we popping open a bottle of champagne, screaming "Yippee!" and celebrating? I couldn't tell him. I just couldn't. I was paralyzed. As progressive and thoughtful as he unfailingly was and, again, as completely egalitarian as our marriage had been, I was inexplicably worried that this money and professional leap would somehow change things in our relationship. It would, somehow, upset our applecart. I worried it would hurt him.

As much as Jim had always lifted me up when I was down, something hard and tight in my gut told me that my news would not make him feel good. I worried that it would upset the natural state of things, the way they were and always should be. So I didn't tell him for two months. Because of exactly how I felt when I did finally tell him. He looked stunned but immediately was congratulatory and happy, of course. As I've emphasized, he's a supportive husband. But I could also tell he was surprised.

And I was shocked by how much it affected me and how guilty I felt. It made me feel as though I'd done something wrong. He did not make me feel this way. On the contrary, he truly seemed proud. But things were different in my head.

DON'T ENJOY, OR "MIXED BAG"

Why did I—why *do* I—feel guilty (if that is even the word)? Looking for some psychological insight, I asked the therapist I most admire and trust, marriage and relationship expert Dr. Jane Greer, what she sees when women start to outearn their spouses. "I've worked with quite a few couples where women have been more successful, either in the scope of their jobs or in greater income and financial status. And it isn't always problematic to begin with. Very often the relationship starts when women are growing their careers and increasing their income potential," she said.

"Oftentimes the competitive issues are more beneath the surface to start—while there may not be overt arguing, you can detect failures in supportive actions and behaviors. Usually partners will like the fact that their spouse is doing well financially, especially if there's a certain equity with access to money and they're both able to spend and enjoy it, enhancing their lifestyles. In that scenario, everybody's happy. However, at some point an element of envy creeps into play around who's doing what, who's making what, and who's calling the shots. That's when the power and the control issues start to flare up."

I never sensed this with Jim, but he doesn't like the way my work monopolizes my mind and my time. He would be much happier with a lot less money and a lot more me.

According to our Working Women Study Poll of male and female breadwinners all across the country, two-thirds (63 percent) of female earners-in-chief say they don't enjoy being the primary earner or that it is a "mixed bag," compared with four in ten male breadwinners (38 percent). Female breadwinners are also less likely than male breadwinners to believe that being the primary earner has a positive effect on their relationships with their spouse/partner. The poll also reports that male breadwinners are more likely to say that being the primary earner has resulted in them having more respect for their spouse/partner. Female breadwinners are more likely to say that having this role has resulted in tension and arguments in the relationship.

And when men and women were asked to respond to various adjectives describing their feelings about being the primary earner "extremely/very well," the results, to me, were astonishing. Consider this chart from the MSNBC Working Women Study Poll:

Adjectives that describe how breadwinners feel about being the primary earner "extremely/very well"

	Female, no kids	Male, no kids	Moms	Dads
Proud	32%	55%	50%	62%
Content	34%	52%	45%	59%
Emotionally Secure	31%	43%	40%	54%
Financially Secure	30%	51%	40%	48%
Empowered	28%	27%	37%	40%
Relieved	19%	31%	27%	39%

There's the heart of the beast, I thought, in big, bold numbers. The majority of male breadwinners, with kids or without, feel really positive about being the primary earner. The majority of women, whether or not they're moms, do not.

When I look at this chart, part of me is completely incredulous. How can we not feel great about finally being at parity with and, in some cases, surpassing men professionally? Even though we know that women in general still earn less on average than their male counterparts, our arrival on the national stage as primary earners should be a call for celebration.

Actually, some women are more apt than others to feel good about that status. According to our survey, female breadwinners are more likely to say they feel "emotionally secure" about being the primary earner if they live in the Northeast

(47 percent) rather than the Midwest (32 percent) or the South (33 percent). The Northeasterner in me understands that. But part of me is also sympathetic to how midwestern and southern women feel. Some of the verbatim responses from women who did not enjoy their role as breadwinner are hard to hear. "I know my spouse would rather support me, than me support him," said one woman. "I do not enjoy the guilt, I do not enjoy the envy," said another.

I do not enjoy the guilt; I do not enjoy the envy. I find that a poignant statement. So many of us seem to come to the table feeling so guilty about everything. Why? Or overly grateful. Why? Feeling guilty that you have kids as well as the job of senior vice president when your husband doesn't make as much money as you. Why? Feeling as though you have to overcompensate as wife and mother when you get home because of the time you spend at work *and* because you make more money. Why? Feeling so grateful that you have this job, that you're not getting the pay you deserve. Why should any of us feel this way?

Again the female breadwinners in our poll put it bluntly and succinctly. "I feel bad for my husband—he says he doesn't mind, but I think he does. I feel responsible for the family by being the main 'breadwinner' and insurance carrier. I wish he was, and not me," one woman said. "I'm proud to make good money as a woman, but it hurts my husband's pride," said another. "Longer hours leave little time for affection," said a female breadwinner, speaking to the exhaustion of work leading to a lack of intimacy in a relationship. Or as another one just came right out with it: "Stress of financial responsibility, spouse's resentfullness [sic] towards me."

But this is the one that jumped off the page for me: "My husband feels like we are in a competition. He says it does not bother him, but I can feel the tension and the competitiveness." I'm sure that my husband doesn't feel competitive with me. But I think Jim feels that he has to compete for my time. That is, it's enough for him that I have so many job-related responsibilities. It's my other projects, my knowing and growing your value work—this book, for example—that he takes issue with. "You're already making enough," he says. "Why are you doing more?" He sees my investment in building this part of my life as an affront to the family. "*That's* more important than *us*?" The questions hurt. The truth hurts.

We had a very serious talk, and his argument was that because I didn't need any more money, then the "extracurricular" part of my career—helping women know and grow their value—must be an exercise in vanity. My response is that of course I don't want to spend more time away from the family; rather, I do this work because I truly believe that I have finally found my calling. And more importantly because I believe I am building a platform that someday our daughters will stand on. In fact, I am doing this, in large part, because I am concerned about our daughters' future as women in this culture and society. I want them to be able to flourish, to be exactly who they are and want to be in all areas of their lives. I also know that my professional value has a "shelf life," and I know I need to save for a more secure future. This all sounds well and good and high-minded, but in Jim's defense, building my brand and name recognition has involved many more red carpet walks, party appearances, and speaking engagements than perhaps this household needed. It took a lot of networking and bad scheduling decisions before this brand was clear and on its way.

When it comes down to it, I think my husband questions the contents of my inner value, which is exactly what I am doing too. He sees this part of my life as needless extra work—vanity, one more reason not to spend time with our family. I see it as my life's work, where my experiences can be of service to a broad range of women. Personally, it's where my professional value and an important aspect of my inner beliefs converge. It makes me feel useful, energized, and happy. It doesn't have a thing to do with my love for him and our family. To be fair, Jim really admires the Know Your Value message, but it was all the things it took to get to this point that didn't make sense to him at all—it leaves too little time for a real family connection.

Which one of us is right? Are either of us right? How do you even define "right" in this context? I don't know, but I'm pretty sure of one thing: I don't think a man building an enterprise would have these problems. Historically, this has to be a new problem. Mothers and wives are needed at home. We are in a bad position when we have to make these choices.

WE DIDN'T ENVISION IT

When I had my big sit-down talk with Dr. Judith Rodin, I asked about her thoughts and experiences on the subject. I felt there was a problem, I said, "as we break through as women, readjusting our own sense of ourselves so that we sell ourselves 'right' to our significant others. Because I think there are problems at home when a woman has professional power and financial success. Would you agree with that?"

Judith agreed immediately and then went even deeper. "Yes, but I think it starts earlier. We're so programmed as young girls and young women to (a) want to be popular and (b) want to find just the right husband or just the right partner, more broadly. And we're willing to present ourselves in ways that we think make the other person like or love us more. That's the young person's 'disease' in a way," she said, interestingly. "It's the insecurity and the immaturity and the lack of life experience that makes you do that.

"I think as women get older and they mature and they go through a period of both personal and professional experiences, they realize that they've got to present themselves to the romantic relationships as 'This is who I am, and if it doesn't work for you, we're not going to work as a pair. It's not that I'm not willing to compromise and do all the things that make any relationship successful, but I am not going to change who I fundamentally am.' That's wisdom and maturity that I wish more young women would have but that may only come with life experience and years. And so if you can help them understand how to incorporate some of that confidence and experience earlier, I think it has the potential to be transformational."

I was fascinated that essentially she characterized people-pleasing as a disease. "How does that 'disease' exhibit itself in

135

relationships and family troubles as a woman grows in her career, do you think?" I asked (and was afraid to hear the answer).

Judith was undaunted. "So in the beginning she's so happy to be in this wonderful relationship and have a partner and feels like she's on her life course on the personal side. And if she starts to develop professional successes, her confidence grows because of those in her working life and her concept of herself. And on this I can not only speak objectively; I'm speaking personally as well that the partner is often—not always, but often—threatened by that. 'This isn't the person I married. This isn't the person I signed on for,'" Judith said. "And the partner's correct! It isn't that person anymore, so they either adjust together to their own transformations—which can happen, and wonderfully so—or they start to grow apart."

But what does that really look like in a partnership or marriage? Examples? "There are the seeds of resentment where small slights become big grievances," Judith continued. "You said you were going to be home at seven, and you were home at nine. And suddenly that's a really big deal where it never would have been before. Because what you were doing in those two hours was something that was such a signal of your professional success and where you are going that it becomes a threat. But the fight isn't *really* over that you were two hours late."

"It's like they become markers of how much you care," I suggested. Judith agreed emphatically. "Exactly! Exactly. And that you are called more than you 'should' be to do what you're doing in your work is sort of reframed as a marker that you're caring less," she ruminated. "So these little things become bigger things. It's the threat around growth and maybe some threat around success."

Boy, did I hear her on that one. You can scream, say it's not fair, even blame it on a stubbornly sexist culture. Still, certain realities persist. If you have achieved some—or a lot—of success in your work life, there are consequences in your personal life. I am aware, for example, that my job takes me away from home quite a bit. I am aware that my husband is alone a lot. I am aware that I am probably moderating a panel during the parent-teacher conference or while my family is eating dinner. I am aware that by always being "on"—a high-gear mental state necessary to do the kind of rapid-speed, multitasking work I do—I am probably making my husband feel as if I'm working my professional "tricks" on him rather than slowing down and remembering who I am and connecting with him as his longtime friend and wife. As I write, it is clear to me that my own nerves and exhaustion are getting in the way of personal success.

When I asked her what that was like for her personally, Judith was frank and thoughtful. "I mean, I have been divorced, and I think that the relationship just couldn't work," she said. "We grew apart because our lives became so different and our success trajectories really diverged, and it was hard for both of us. He resented me, and I think I unintentionally demeaned him because he wasn't going as fast as I was. So I think we were both guilty." Then, she added, "And it's so real. Just watch out for the little things that he picks on you for, because that's such a sign of where and how he's threatened. But on the optimistic side, I have since been happily married now for twenty years, to a real professional and intellectual partner who is my biggest fan."

I'm on live television in the morning for three hours. Then, while my husband is at work, there could be something about me on the Internet; in our age of tweeting, blogging, and gawking, the buzzfeed is relentless, glamorizing, demeaning, always "on." Then I'm on stage giving a speech, and there are pictures in the paper, on the web. I'm getting clothes thrown at me to wear on television or at events; I get gifts, tickets, and special invitations all the time. VIP treatment. I'm writing books and revealing a lot of my own life in the process. I feel that, to Jim—and he's probably right—my job description has changed from "reporter" to "media personality" and that my work life has become celebritized. And celebrity doesn't fly in our house. With anybody. Not even the dog is impressed.

I wondered about this aloud with Judith. "I feel like in some ways it's natural for that feeling of threat to happen. Do you think that's true?" I asked. "I don't think we've ever seen so many women do so professionally well before. And maybe it isn't just that the men may be threatened, but that maybe we didn't envision this dynamic either."

She jumped on it immediately. "Wait, when you say 'we didn't envision it,' I want to stop there because I think that's really important. You know, lots of us did well in high school and college, and we get to some point in our career and we ask ourselves: Can I *envision* what all of this is?" Judith said. "I remember sitting at my desk at Yale my first year there as an assistant professor . . . but I was fearful. I was waiting to be 'found out' that I wasn't as smart as everybody thought. I wasn't as creative as everybody thought. I have to say that I think a lot of women in the beginning both aspire but also are fearful. I know that was the case with me."

But then, Judith said, she hit her stride. "For me, the turning point both maritally and in that feeling was that seven or eight years out after [my first year at Yale] I both won the American Psychological Association Early Career Award, which they give to a young person in psychology who they feel at the early part of their career has really super-distinguished themselves, and I got tenure at Yale. All in the same year," she recalled. "It was amazing, and I realized I didn't fear getting 'found out' anymore. But things were getting worse at home. And they were certainly correlated."

THIS IS WHO I AM

Striking the right balance between communicating your energy and willingness to do the job as well as your personal style and passion is not just the first step in launching your career as a young woman, an entrepreneur, or both; it's also the first step in growing your professional and inner value. It's where you, as a package, cohere and make a good first impression on the world. It's also a way to strengthen your sense of yourself and your capabilities. It's about not only being a team player but also being true to yourself. In that regard, there will perhaps be no proving ground more intense than that of personal relationships. And as you start your career and life, getting your relationship off to the right start—being clear about who you are with your boyfriend, girlfriend, or partner from the start—is critical.

It's simply too important to ignore. If you are ambitious for yourself, for your career, you've got to be clear about that in your personal life—and certainly with the person with whom you plan on spending it. If you can look a prospective employer in the eye and communicate what you bring to the table and what you're willing to do, you should definitely be able to do that with your partner.

I think women need to come to this conclusion a lot earlier in life. This is a conclusion that entrepreneur Amanda Steinberg, founder and CEO of the women's financial media site DailyWorth.com, also came to after years of thinking she wanted something else in her relationships. During a conversation at her home in Philadelphia she said that the kind of life that had been marketed to her as a girl and young woman involved being "saved" by a man. When that hadn't happened by the time she reached her early thirties, Amanda realized that a big part of the reason was because she hadn't been clear enough with herself that, in fact, that wasn't what she wanted.

"About a year or so after I started my company, I was on my own, and I went through a period of being really lonely. But during that time I realized that I was okay being my own rock, that it would be great to be in a stimulating, nurturing relationship, but that I was never going to be okay with it if it meant I had to pretend I was someone I wasn't," she said. "And who I was and am is a very focused entrepreneur, driven by mission and ambition to take on the idea that women want to take charge of their financial lives and, therefore, their destinies—that we don't need someone to do that for us."

In her current relationship Amanda feels fully embraced for who she is authentically. "I feel seen and appreciated for who I actually am, and a lot of that is because my boyfriend is someone who understands and loves that, but it's also because I developed the strength to be as direct with him about what makes me tick as I am with our investors and community about the guiding principles and goals of the company," she said. "Does it mean that I'm always this bulwark of strength; an island? No. But it makes me a more conscious partner because now that I can feel comfortable in my own skin with my partner, I can be open to who he is and what he needs too."

Still, I'm not saying that this is easy. I know that in my own life it hasn't been easy. Had I always been transparent about my ambition with my husband? I thought I had. But maybe I hadn't. Maybe I couldn't do that until I'd had the experience to know who I was in terms of my professional value and my inner value. Maybe I wouldn't have felt as though my professional value and my inner value were so detached from each other if I had been more honest about who I was and what I wanted from life. Maybe that was the source of the tension in my marriage. Maybe Judith is right: being able to know and articulate who you are—that is, to know and grow your own professional and inner value—is a byproduct of maturity.

The subject came up during my conversation with Senator Claire McCaskill. I wanted to know whether she thought there was any prescription or warning we could give young women about choosing a partner. I didn't know what the advice should be except that women definitely need to choose someone who they think will grow with them—and I was not sure that was an easy thing to do. Senator McCaskill was very wise on the topic. Her advice was straightforward, outlining the chain of events likely to take place if you aren't honest in your relationship.

"I think to some extent [telling young women they need to be honest about their ambition] puts a lot of pressure on young women who hear that, and some of that pressure is unnecessary. But I do think you have to know what you enjoy doing and drive toward it and then use that as your armor to try to foster your ambition," she said. "For example, if you figure out you're in a job and you've got five different jobs you do, and three of them you hate and two of them you love, then you've got to immediately start reminding every-body how good you are at the two you love so that you will then be seen as someone who can continue to excel in those areas, and in that way I think even very young women in their careers can begin branding themselves."

But, Senator McCaskill pointed out, this can be easier said than done while managing a serious relationship or marriage. "I'm divorced and remarried, so I would never be so phony as to say that my career and my ambition have never been an issue in my personal or family life. Of course they have," she said. "But I will say, in my marriage—and frankly that door swings both ways—that some of this was my fault. I'm not about to say that I have been a victim here. Sometimes my first husband was a victim because I was not as thoughtful as I should have been at very important times. So I learned a lot from my failures in my first marriage in addition to some things I thought didn't work from his perspective."

She also pointed out the clearest way to know when your professional and personal lives are out of whack. "If you feel like you are way out of balance in terms of your work versus personal life, you need to look at your personal life and see if you're gravitating toward work because you're not happy in your personal life. And you've got to fix your personal life. It's not going to get better by just consuming yourself, just totally getting so into work," Senator McCaskill continued. "What I found myself doing, rather than the hard work that is required in a marriage . . . was just saying 'Well, I've got to work,' or 'I've got this big job. I'm the elected prosecutor in Kansas City. I'm running all this office—I've got all these felonies!' And I just pulled myself away and justified it because of all the work I had to do. And I think men historically have done this a lot. If things are out of balance, then examine your personal life and make sure that you are in a good place, that you are happy there. . . . If you're not happy at work, you're going to want to stay home. If you're not happy at home, you're going to want to stay at work. So if you are going to get a balance, you've got to be happy both places."

Senator McCaskill's story made me sad. Like Judith Rodin, the senator had pointed out that her dedication to her career had, in important ways, negatively impacted her marriage. She had ducked out of her relationship to focus on work, when the marriage seemed too difficult to face. As so many women seem to do, she brought up the subject of "balance," but to me the question of how to integrate one's professional and inner lives is not so much one of balance. Powerhouse PepsiCo CEO Indra Nooyi—who you will read more about in the next chapter—believes that the key to her successful thirty-five years of marriage has been her ability to compartmentalize the many sides of herself. She has subtracted part of herself from the home equation, trying not to bring her work self past the garage. Her version of "balance" seems to be keeping the different parts of her life separate . . . and it actually appears to be working. Yet I think balance is a bourgeois illusion, one that is marketed to guilty, over-stressed working women who cleave to the idea that an even, bump-free life is available to them if they would only buy these yoga clothes or microwave this frozen meal or take those meds.

You may not have read it here first, but consider this the last word on the subject: there *is* no balance. You will have to make significant sacrifices, so make your peace with it. Knowing that early on, as a young woman—or as an entrepreneur whose life is, by definition, full of work-life trade-offs—is vital if you are going to build a truly successful life. To me the question of how to do that is one of knowing yourself, of wrapping your mind and spirit around the value you bring to the marketplace and the value you bring to your personal life. Being able to articulate and to embody both is the essence of growing your overall brand—the whole package that is your life.

"YOUR" MONEY

According to our poll, four in ten (39 percent) female bread-winners say there is more tension in their relationship because they are the primary earner, compared with one in five (21 percent) male breadwinners. One in five female breadwinners (19 percent) reports that being the primary earner has had a negative impact on their marriage/relationship, compared with only 5 percent of male breadwinners. Three in ten female breadwinners say they have had arguments with their spouse/partner over the balance of power in their relationship. One in six says that it has threatened their relationship.

My husband and I have never argued about the balance of power in our relationship since my raise. The less we talk about work, the better. The only person I can talk about power dynamics with is usually only another woman in my position, one who also makes more money than her husband. Because that woman will understand—even if it isn't the case in her own relationship—she'll get it. No one wants to touch it for fear that the whole apparatus will crumble apart on impact. I think it's probably true of many breadwinning women. And because of that, I agree with Judith that it's natural that many find themselves slowly growing apart from their mates because of the demands and realities of their actual careers. But for me it's the financial piece that makes me nervous. I was not prepared for that. And again, it was my own issue with it that caused these problems—the guilt I felt about it, the guilt I felt about what it took to get there, the sacrifices I made at home to advance my career, my salary, and my children's future.

Of course, as an educated, career-oriented woman, I always aspired to bring home the bacon. I loved the concept of being able to provide for my family. But I did not think, when I surpassed my husband in numbers, that it was going to mean living with so much loaded silence around the issue. I think many of us live this way. I know my experience is probably a bit more public and exaggerated version of what many women feel like when their earning capital exceeds their husbands', but the net result is the same. It's a power shift that I don't think anyone in the household is ready for.

Certainly we weren't. Almost right away the language changed. When he made the bigger salary, we used to talk about "our" money; our combined income was a marital asset. When I started making more, Jim started referring to it as "your money." It just happened. He never stormed in one evening and growled, "This doesn't work for me, you pulling in more money than I do. I feel like this is not 'our' money; that's *your* money, and I will not be made to feel inferior!" He would never dream of doing or saying anything even remotely like this. I'm sure if I were to ask him if he did, in fact, feel that way or something along those lines, he would say it was ridiculous.

Yet the money conversation has changed. I still think of our money as a marital asset, but if, for example, he wants to buy something, he'll seem guilty and say, "I don't want to take your money." Whenever we're thinking about making a big purchase or taking a trip, Jim will say something like, "I'm not sure if we should spend so much of your money on that." That little shift from "our" to "your" has had a tectonic effect on the balance of power in our relationship, the way our household is run, and the way we communicate.

It's evidently not too loaded for other women to talk about, though. "I am responsible for all the bills. Because of that, I make sure I make all the decisions about the household, and he doesn't like that, so that causes some friction," reported one woman in our poll. When I read that, I could feel my heart pop like a soap bubble. *That's not Jim and me—right?* Having said that, Jim would say—and has said—that I have changed as a person, while I, however, always looked at it as growing and securing our family's future. We may both be right. It doesn't seem fair, but we definitely may both be right.

A LITTLE BIT LIKE A PARTNERSHIP

Incredibly, for some couples money and power dynamics just don't seem to matter all that much. Being a breadwinner, no matter who it is, makes for a more relaxed dynamic in their relationship. To be clear, such people represent a minority: in our poll only 8 percent of female and 24 percent of male primary earners say there is *less* tension in the household as a result of them being the breadwinner. And you can feel the lack of tension from the laissez-faire tone of their comments, verbatim from our poll. "As long as we have income coming in, it doesn't matter who's making more," said one woman. From a woman grateful to have fewer fights with her spouse over money concerns: "My becoming the primary earner has meant more money for us overall, so finances are less tight. Less financial worries equal less tension." One reported a benefit: "The household duties are now done by my partner with no complaints, and I don't have to deal with the stuff that I don't like to do."

Any one of these comments could have come out of the mouth of Dee Dee Myers, who was White House press secretary during the first two years of the Clinton administration and is now executive vice president for Worldwide Corporate Communications and Public Affairs at Warner Bros. I was talking to her on the phone from her (then) new home in LA when, curious, I asked her how it felt for her to be her family's primary earner.

I could practically hear her shrug. "I don't think about it very much, and I don't think he really cares," she said. "In the course of our marriage we have sort of traded back and forth, depending on who is doing what, and how flexible one is versus the other, depending on what's going on. That's always worked really well for us . . . [and] Todd does all the cooking."

Wow. I hinted that it wasn't going so easily for me, maybe because I was a newbie. "I sometimes feel guilty about it," I said. "I don't know why. It's kind of a weird, new thing for me. Sounds like you guys have always had an evolving [breadwinner status]."

Dee Dee thought about it. "No, I think we always look at it a little bit like a partnership, almost like everything goes into the partnership, and some of it is monetary, and some equity . . . and Todd makes my life so much more interesting. How do you put a value on that?" she mused. "You know what the other thing is? Neither of us cares that much about money. We are responsible with that money, but we have never had a fight over money. Not once." And they've been married almost eighteen years. What in the world was their secret?

Again I could almost hear the shrug. "[My husband] just doesn't really care. He doesn't need a lot. Like, it would never occur to him to buy an expensive car. He drives the minivan.

And I drive an SUV," Dee Dee said bluntly. "He's much more interested in things that have historic value as opposed to monetary value, that have an emotional value . . . like the art projects that he made in third grade." Dee Dee said that, of course, they talked about moving, selling their house, buying a new one—that sort of thing. "But it's never, 'You can't spend this much money on a pair of shoes,'" she said. "Or . . . 'You can't buy a first edition of the Great Gatsby.'" And there it was. I couldn't believe it: the subject of money was emotionally irrelevant to them.

But it turns out there are those couples who one-up people like Dee Dee and her husband: they're actually happy with the wife being the breadwinner.

WE COMMUNICATE MORE EFFECTIVELY

According to the MSNBC Working Women Study poll, although female breadwinners are less likely than male breadwinners to believe being the primary earner has a positive effect on their relationship with their spouse/partner, there is a small minority of women—16 percent—who report that it has been great. For these women communication and work-life balance with their partners has actually improved since they became the household breadwinners. Also, perhaps because there is generally less tension in households where money isn't scarce, our survey reports that female breadwinners with higher household incomes are more likely than those with lower household incomes to say they enjoy being the primary earner (43 percent household income

$75,000+ versus 33 percent household income under $50,000). Specifically, these women are more likely to express positive sentiments such as "content" (54 percent women with household income $100,000+), "emotionally secure" (51 percent), "financially secure" (58 percent), and "empowered" (44 percent).

Consider this chart from the poll on that 16 percent:

Reasons being the primary earner has had a positive impact on intimate life
(asked of those who said very/somewhat positive)

	Female breadwinners who say positive impact on intimate life (16% of total)	Total female breadwinners
We communicate more effectively and openly, which makes us closer	55%	9%
Since I'm in the "financial driver's seat," my spouse/partner appreciates me more and is more attentive	39%	6%
I'm turned on by how open-minded and secure my partner/spouse is about my status as the primary earner	33%	5%

Certainly I have a lot to learn from this small but incredible group of women. Maybe many of us do. Somehow they, and women like them whom we didn't get to poll, have managed to construct lives in such a way that their success at work isn't interfering with their relationships. In fact, it's just the opposite: it's apparently enhancing them. Read this comment from a primary-earning woman, verbatim from the survey: "I feel a sense of accomplishment and pride, especially in today's world. That said, it's always a team effort, regardless of the income."

These women seem to have hit the sweet spot where their professional value and inner value grow in tandem. Who in the world are they?

Bobbi Brown, cosmetics mogul, for one. It came up during our conversation about growing your value. When I asked her whether she was married, Bobbi replied that she was. "I am happily married," she said. "Happily married for twenty-six years." I did a verbal double take: "Did you just say *happily*?" She confirmed. "I did. I am happily married. I adore my husband." She gave some sweet background. "My husband has his own business—he's a real estate developer and an attorney," she explained. "And now, especially since my kids are getting older, we remember why we actually enjoy being together. We like the same things."

I love hearing happy endings like this, and I want that for myself. But I wanted to know from Bobbi whether hers was the result of hard work in the marriage, especially as her business grew. "Did you experience any challenges when your career took off?" I asked. "The answer doesn't have to be yes."

But Bobbi was emphatic. "Absolutely! Absolutely. There's always challenges [*sic*], and for me, personally, figuring out how to balance was really difficult. The truth is there's no such thing as balance. But my husband was really helpful when I was overloaded and exhausted and kind of freaked out that I had to travel to promote my business or be at certain events," she said. "He would say to me, 'Stop. Breathe. Think about what you're doing. You don't have to do everything. Do it your way and do what matters.'" And what had really mattered to her? "Our family always mattered more than being at every single event," she said.

What a powerful example of a life in which professional value and inner value dovetail beautifully! And it was clearly the dynamic between Bobbi and her husband that had, in large part, made that life possible. But how, I wanted to know, had he responded to her ambition? "Well, we started the brand together. When we started the brand, I was a freelance makeup artist, and he was in law school. We started together with just ten lipsticks," she recalled. "We never thought about the big picture. We certainly never thought about where it would be today. We always just thought about what *is*. That's how I've always lived my life, and I still do actually."

PROVIDER PRIDE

Not really thinking about who is making more money. Not looking at the big picture. Going with today. These are the modus operandi of a couple of very successful, ambitious women who make more money than their husbands. It makes me wonder: Am I *creating* these problems around money and power with my husband? He's never been anything but supportive of my career; maybe he really just wants to see more of me. Is it possible that this is all in my head?

I had a revelation about this talking with *Glamour* editor-in-chief Cindi Leive about her feelings about being the breadwinner in her household. Cindi had clearly done some thinking about it. "It took me a while to really be able to have what I think of as 'provider pride'—you know, that feeling that I am actually doing something positive and wonderful for my family," she said. "And of course, when you say it objectively, you know, it's like, 'Yeah duh . . . of *course* you are going to be proud of that.' But I think for a lot of women it feels like something selfish. You have to be able to bask in that. To be able to do that in this economy as a woman or a man is a great thing."

Selfish. Bask. I wanted to unpack those words and the thoughts behind them. I felt like I was going to get the key to something resembling an answer. "And do you let yourself bask in that? Do you feel guilty?" I asked. "Because I have to say, for me, it was a really weird transition and a weird power that I did not expect or actually . . . want. I don't know if 'power' is the right word, but all of a sudden everyone in my family turned to me for every decision. Is your advice to . . . expect that that could happen in your life? To be ready for that? How do you make it work?"

Cindi was philosophical. "I guess that my first advice is marry somebody who would be as psyched about [you being the breadwinner] as you would, and I guess that is easier said than done. But I do feel like fundamentally, if you're in a relationship with someone who is grudging about your career success or feels that it comes at the expense of their own, I think it's probably hard to overcome that," she said.

(On reflection I have to say that although I do agree with Cindi that women need to figure out whether they've got the right partner before the wedding or otherwise life commitment, I don't think you can always tell by what a potential life partner might say to you about his feelings concerning salary inequity. I do, however, think that it's essential for women to be very clear with themselves as well as their love interests about who they are and what their intended trajectory is—and to not soften their ambitions to make themselves or their partners less insecure. Tell the truth to your partner and to yourself. It only backfires if you don't, because it's basically impossible to squelch your true nature.)

"My husband, I guess, he's just always been very fully accepting of it. And he's been proud of me, so then it's easier for me to be proud of myself," Cindi said.

I thought about that for a moment. "My husband is too. I think sometimes it's in our heads," I said. "I love your advice. Bask in it. Have provider pride." Maybe my needless guilt over making more money had made me think there were problems in my marriage because of it! Maybe in this case I am the one standing in the way of merging my professional value and inner value. Maybe it's closer than I think.

And that may be true. But there is a group of people whose feelings, without question, can become very real, very complex, and sometimes very angry as a result of any professional woman's ambition and hard-earned successes.

Those people are your children.

CHAPTER SIX

"LEAVE YOUR CROWN IN THE GARAGE"

How Powerful Women Subjugate Themselves at Home to Keep the Peace

One year I was reporting a story on the road, which, as a TV journalist, I often do. This time, though, the day of my return home from the work trip happened to coincide with the evening of the year's most important parent-teacher conference. Well, my work being what it often is, I didn't get home as planned. There was more news to cover, and Joe and I had to stay. Period.

But I was panicking. It was critical that I attend this meeting. Never mind that my husband couldn't make it either, also for work-related reasons. The mother wasn't going to be there. I knew how devastated my daughter would be that I was—for the kazillionth time—missing one of her important life events because my job called me away. I was hundreds of miles away and working through the night. I cringed so deeply thinking about it that it physically hurt. What was I going to do? Finally I came up with an idea. I sneaked away, called up my wonderful manager/executive assistant, Emily Cassidy, who then sped to the school with her phone, just in time for me to FaceTime (videophone) in and join the meeting.

It wasn't the greatest solution (I don't think I necessarily impressed her teacher). But it was the best I could do under the circumstances, and the meeting went well. Things did not, however, go well with my daughter. When I got home, I was treated to a lot of sassy backtalk. Unacceptably sassy back-talk. And instead of saying and doing what I, as a good mother, should have said and done—"You may not talk to your mother that way, young lady," and sending her to her room—I crumpled in guilt. Sometimes the overly modulated, exaggerated attempts to "be there" or "do it all" leave the very people you are home to "be there" for, cold. The FaceTime thing made it all about me, showing the world that I could do everything. Enough!

Judging from the national survey conducted for this book, it sounds as if many breadwinning mothers are feeling that way, more or less. Not that we necessarily know what being a "good mom" means exactly, anyway. Before we get into the good news about working mothers and their families in the next chapter, we're going to start with the mixed bag in this one. There are many ways in which being an attentive, attached mom doesn't contraindicate a demanding career, but let's face it: there are also many ways in which it does.

According to our poll on breadwinners and their relation-ships, fathers are more likely to say that marital and parental roles are clearer because they are the primary earner, whereas mothers are more likely to say that these roles are more complicated as a result of their primary-earner status. Breadwinner moms are also less likely than breadwinner dads to say that being the primary earner has had a positive effect on their relationship with their children: 36 percent versus 52 percent. Breadwinner moms are twice as likely as breadwinner dads to say, "I'm exhausted on all fronts; I never get a break" (43 percent versus 19 percent). Nearly half of breadwinner moms agree with the statement, "I feel guilty that I can't be there for them like the stay-at-home-parents, and I can see that this alienates me from my children to some degree," compared with just under a third of breadwinner dads. Read: shopping spree.

Findings like this, to me, basically reveal what any mother who is also a hard-working professional already knows: we're exhausted, stressed, lonely. *And* we are wracked with guilt when we come home and try to embrace the angry, distant, rude, or extremely demanding children that we only get to see for a few hours every day. If that. We're lonely, guilty, and defensive on weekends, when, if we want to watch our kids' soccer games, we're face to face with the neighborhood SAHM posse—the domestic goddess cult who, in an era of intensive attachment parenting, has already judged and convicted us of being neglectful, absentee mothers. And it doesn't help that most of our fellow Americans don't support us. As mentioned earlier, according to a 2013 Pew study, only 16 percent of those Americans polled thought that a home with the mother working full-time was the best environment in which to raise a child. That's pretty damning, considering that most mothers work. So thanks for that, America.

The whole proposition of being a breadwinning or career-driven mother is murky, sticky, and messy.

THESE WOMEN ARE SUCCEEDING, BUT THEY DON'T FEEL THEY ARE

"The dilemmas of working and parenthood . . . start the moment we become mothers—identities formed through careers are forced to incorporate the new role of 'mommy,'" wrote Tovah Klein, PhD, director of the Barnard College Center for Toddler Development and associate professor of psychology in 2014. "Identity-turmoil gets sparked: Am I a career woman? Ambitious person? Mother? This can be followed by a path of 'Who am I?' that can take years to resolve."

No kidding! In my experience "ambitious person" and "mother" blend about as well as oil and vinegar. Indeed, in a qualitative study that Klein and her colleagues conducted of 240 women who had careers before becoming mothers, researchers found that "the resounding message is that they feel they are not doing enough—for their careers (whether currently employed or not) or their children, and are torn between the clashing domains. . . . They struggle to do-it-all at one moment. Even though many desire to [*sic*]. In fact, by most objective measures these women are succeeding, but they don't feel they are."

These women are succeeding, but they don't feel they are. That sentence sums up perfectly for me the struggle imbedded in my psyche and, I'll bet, that of many career-driven mothers. Working motherhood is where my professional value and inner value clash most cruelly. My persona as a professional news broadcaster embraces qualities such as a hard-driving work ethic, politesse, tough-mindedness, ease with public speaking, and quick on-the-feet performance. The essence of my identity as a mother involves—or at least I want it to—being comforting, nurturing, a good listener, a judicious disciplinarian. But a weird hybrid often pops out when I try to force these two together: a "go, go!" mom who implodes on impact. The pieces just don't fit together right somehow.

Dads just don't have this problem, to this degree. Experience says it. Research says it. But if a woman has achieved some—or a lot of—success in her work life, it's easy for her to feel constantly reminded of her deficiencies as a mother and to feel conflicted about the balance of power in the household. According to our poll, male breadwinners are three times as likely as female breadwinners to say that there is less tension in the relationship (24 percent men versus 8 percent women), whereas three in ten (29 percent) female breadwinners report having had arguments with their spouse/partner over the "balance of power" in the relationship, compared with one in five male breadwinners (20 percent). And women are more likely to report arguments about the balance of power if they have children under eighteen (34 percent), compared with those with no children (22 percent).

Part of me wants to scream that it's not fair that our culture is still so sexist. But the persistent reality is that I am almost constantly aware of how my career disrupts our household. I am reminded either by my family's behavior (or by teachers, stay-at-home moms, grandmothers—including my own mother) or by my own hypercritical self-awareness.

I am aware, for example, that my job takes me away from home a lot. (Bad mom.) I am aware that my husband and daughters are alone a lot—or at least without me. (Bad mom.) I am aware that I am probably moderating a panel or giving a speech at an event during the parent-teacher conference. (Bad mom.) I am aware that my always being "on"—a high-gear mental state necessary to do the kind of rapid-speed, multi-tasking work I do—makes my kids feel as if I'm working my professional bag of tricks on them rather than slowing down and remembering who I am and connecting with them as their mother.

I have addressed this problem in many ways. I overcompensate by going on shopping sprees with my daughters, taking the family on exciting vacations (during which I'm rabidly checking my texts and e-mails), and by being sugary sweet and irritatingly upbeat when I'm at home. But, of course, overcompensating doesn't bring you closer to those you're trying to please. They sniff out the forgery and retreat from you further. That is what I have learned the hard way: kids want parameters, expectations. I need to be a parent, no matter what they think of me. This approach has worked, but it has also made me more lonely, if possible.

When I spoke with Senator Claire McCaskill, she knew all about the secret dual lives of moms and professional working women. Truly, as she spoke, I felt as if she were describing my life. Verbatim. "I was in the courtroom asking someone to put someone away for fifty years for a horrendous crime, and I was rushing home so that I would not have to serve takeout for the fourth night in a row and killing myself so that my kids would have meatloaf and mashed potatoes for dinner that I had mashed myself and not used a box. And I did that all the time. It was just normal for me to do those kinds of things," she said of her years as a prosecutor when her children were young.

"I was single, with my children, for almost a decade when they were little, and then you really have a lot of guilt. . . . My kids were smart enough—I think all kids are smart enough—to know what to use to manipulate. And what they would use was my guilt. All they had to do was go close to, 'Well, you know *other* moms were at this, and you weren't,' and then I was like, 'Oh my God, what can I do? What can I do? What can I do *for* you? What can I do *with* you?' So as a parent I probably made some serious parenting mistakes by allowing that guilt manipulation way too many times. But I did."

I got it completely. To lead the bizarre, bifurcated life of a high-powered working mother—rushing home from a professional, pressurized, demanding work environment to a home where your kids are, however justifiably, sick of takeout and your phoniness—is a tall order. And that raises what, to me, is the central question: How can mothers stay authentically themselves at home and with their children? Is it even possible to feel successful as a mother with an ambitious career?

ONE MOUTH AND MANY, MANY EARS

"Leave your crown in the garage." That's what PepsiCo CEO Indra Nooyi's mother told her when she got the big promotion. As head of one of the most iconic companies in the world, Indra Nooyi is one of the most powerful people in business, period. But unlike CEOs like Sheryl Sandberg and others—who acknowledge that being a good mom and a hard-driving professional is hard, but that it's vital that women continue to lean in to their careers—Indra flat-out tells it like it is: being successful as a mom and a hard-driving, career-minded person is only possible when you are two people. And maybe not even then.

When she was asked whether women can "have it all" at the elite 2014 Aspen Ideas Festival, Indra declared bluntly in front of a live audience that "having it all" was difficult, something that women "*pretend* we have," she said. She went on to confess that working mothers don't just "die with guilt" over their children, but to pull off being a working mother "you have to co-opt a lot of people to help you," she said. "But if you ask our daughters, I'm not sure they will say that I've been a good mom. I'm not sure."

Indra and I sat down to a long talk after I had moderated the White House panel and she had spoken at Aspen. I shared the Awkward Moment I'd had at the White House Summit when the room went silent after I'd asked the panel whether they had experienced any stress in their home lives because of their careers. Indra got it right away. "Totally, totally. I think it's partially true for men, but definitely true for women, and every woman CEO or every woman senior executive—there's pain behind that job. Trade-offs you've made, what you've gone through," she said candidly. "My mom always said, 'the moment you enter the house, you are not the CEO. If you want to be a successful mom and a wife, leave your crown in the garage. Just don't bring the crown in.'" Her *mother* had told her that? Indra nodded. It reminded me of something Senator McCaskill had said to me during our conversation. "I need the love and the sustenance of my family—I need it like I need oxygen," she said, tearing up thinking about how much they meant to her. "So if you can't figure out how to make sure *that* is good, you can't go soaring as high as you think you can soar." To feel successful at home and at work, I felt that Claire was saying, you have to adapt your own attitudes, behaviors, and maneuvers until you feel you have the wind under your wings—or else you'll crash. What Indra was saying, essentially, was that to be successful as a wife and mother as well as a career-driven person, you have to be two different people.

She underlined this point. "You have to be. You know, it's interesting: at work we force people to bring their whole selves to work. We try to create an environment at work so that they don't have to leave themselves at the door—we are very particular about that at PepsiCo," Indra observed. "But at home, if I can retain 20 percent of my CEOship and drop 80 percent of it, I have to do it. I *have* to do it. Otherwise—I've been married thirty-five years—I couldn't have kept the marriage going."

How did she keep it going, and how did she manage to be such a calm mother at home when her work obligations were creeping into her mind? "You get up at four in the morning when everybody is asleep. And by six a.m. you get things done so that when everybody gets up, you're smiling, and you say, 'Hi, how are you?' So you have to develop your coping mechanism." Before I had a chance to comment—*wow, what a strategy*—Indra continued. "I think if you talk to any woman CEO, they're doing that—and then you give up a lot of your personal life," she commented. "I love going to ball games—I don't go to those. I love watching concerts. I watch them on DVD at home. Because there's no time to do those things."

There was that sexist double standard, popping up again. "But men have time," I insisted. "Men CEOs have time." Indra agreed. "Yeah, they do have time. Sometimes I ask myself the question . . . if Dad was a CEO, would the kids all behave differently?" she mused. "But Mom CEO? You're a CEO, but you're mom first." I wondered what this looked like on the ground. That is, what mysterious, supernatural force did she have to undergo in the time between leaving her CEO self at work and slipping into her mom self at home? "I have one mouth and many, many ears [at home]," Indra explained. Was she really telling herself to shut up when her kids said or did something that made her want to yell—in order to keep the peace for *her*, to keep steady in both domestic and professional worlds? This was, for me, a jaw-dropping moment. For one thing, Indra was talking openly about accepting her dual life as CEO and mom. For another, I completely related to it.

I often feel as though I have no authority to put my foot down at home because I'm not there often enough to deserve it. I let my kids' bad behavior go because I feel guilty. My crown is definitely checked at the front door. And I too am often thinking of work—although I don't do as good a job of disguising it as Indra does. Clearly. My daughters can tell when my mind has left the room. They know when they're trying to engage with a mannequin mom, and they hate it. By the time I've snapped out of it, the moment to connect has often passed. It's those lost moments—those little windows that can open to mother-child closeness—that I most regret. What did Indra most regret? What, if anything, would she have done differently? Anything she could share with other women?

Instead of answering my questions, she told a story. "I have to tell you, I came to PepsiCo, and my daughter was nine months old—my second daughter. And my older daughter was nine years old. Difficult ages. And I worked twenty hours a day, seven days a week because PepsiCo was going through a lot of changes," Indra recounted. "And my little one was here in the office the other day, and I said, 'Tara, when we move . . . all this furniture is going away.' She said, 'No, we're going to buy this table!' I said, 'Why are we buying this table?' She said, 'The little cubby hole under the table—that's where I used to sleep in the evenings! You can't give that away, Mom! That was my bedroom many times.'"

Her office desk was her baby's bedroom? Indra confirmed. "This is the same table I got the day I started at PepsiCo twenty years ago. I have not changed it; I have kept the same furniture," she said. "And underneath that is a cubby hole where you put your feet in. Tara would walk in with her security blanket, and she'd go underneath that and curl up and sleep.

"And my older daughter, her journal entries made me choke up. 'Waited to talk to mom. It's 10 p.m. Going to bed. Mom not home as yet.'"

Indra's story spoke epics about life for working mothers and small children. I completely related to her experience, almost to the letter. When I was an anchor at CBS, my girls used to crawl under my desk during live broadcasts. I couldn't figure out a way to integrate my work life and motherhood, so bringing them with me and letting them cuddle around my feet while I read the news was my solution. And it was fun. When they were little.

"There is one thing I would do differently," said Indra, finally answering the question. "Perhaps spent a lot more time with the kids." It was a poignant admission that I connected with completely. Indra didn't feel as though she could have progressed in her career had she not put in full-court effort at the office, but doing so was necessarily at the expense of being with her children. Actually she didn't just *feel* that way; she knew it was true, she said. "I honestly believe women, especially twenty years ago, started in a hole. Did not matter how good you were. You had to dig out of the hole, and then excel, so we had to work twice as much," she argued. "This level playing field is a more recent development. Twenty years ago you always had to work hard, whether we liked it or not."

What conflicting messages I was getting from some of the most senior women in the country on inner value versus professional value! On the one hand, Judith Rodin and Claire McCaskill had told me that their marriages and family lives had taken a backseat to their careers—and that's what had

made their professional lives work. On the other hand, PepsiCo's powerhouse CEO was telling me she became submissive
at home to make her family life and marriage work. Was anyone right? Isn't there some middle ground where you can
succeed at work *and* still have a solid personal life?

SENDING ME A SIGNAL

If you want to excel, you always have to work hard, whether
your kids like it or not. And let's clearly acknowledge that for
the majority of the world's mothers, whether to work hard or
not—or whether or not anyone likes it—isn't up for debate.
In the United States alone just over a quarter of all households
are headed by single mothers who are the primary or sole
earners. We know that as of 2013, 40 percent of all American
households are supported by a breadwinning mom who is
either the primary or sole earner—and where our relationships with our children are concerned, that status takes its toll
on a fair number of us.

According to our own poll, more than one-third of breadwinner moms say they "feel as though I'm not there for my
kids as much as I feel I should," compared with one-fourth of
breadwinner dads—and the agreement is higher among
breadwinner moms who are the sole earner (55 percent).
Breadwinner moms are also more likely to say that being the
primary earner has had a negative impact on their relationship with their children if they are the sole earner (24 percent), compared with those who are not the sole earner (9
percent). You can hear the range of realities and emotions in

the voices of some of those women from our poll. "It has taken me away from my children. Children need their mother, regardless of money. But they cannot have their needs met if I don't work," said one woman. "It's very stressful having to carry the financial weight in the relationship. Someone is always counting on you, when you have no one you can count on financially," said another.

But what about mothers who love their work and are ambitious to succeed in their fields, but don't necessarily "need" to do so for financial reasons? For those women, Indra had argued, it is a choice between working hard rather than spending more time with their children—whether they like it or not. And it begs the terrible question: Is it okay to choose to work hard rather than spend extra time with your kids, even though you have regrets or wish that you didn't have to make a choice to begin with? At heart this is the question the White House panel hadn't wanted to answer.

In truth probably no mother can answer it absolutely affirmatively. But after the summit (off stage) Dr. Judith Rodin had spoken to me about her experiences as a mother and tenured Yale professor, working her way up in her career and on to becoming the president of University of Pennsylvania, the first woman to do so at an Ivy League school. There was no getting away from having a constant pit in your stomach if you felt disconnected from your children, she said, nor was there any way around your kids feeling bad if they feel disconnected from you.

"I think that's a very common experience, and I think that the truth is [that] the more disconnected your family is feeling from you too, you are not only *giving* that feedback, but you are getting that feedback *back*. And that makes it harder [because] sometimes they're overt," Judith pointed out. Perhaps if the kids are young enough or have a close enough attachment to us, they'll give us very clear signals that they need their moms. Now. We might be able and want to give them our full attention. But other times we have to work—or might actually be doing something for ourselves.

Judith illustrated this point by describing her experiences with her then-young son. "I remember I was at home and I was playing with my three- or four-year-old—I forget how old he was—and the phone rang, and he dashed to answer it. It was obviously either a colleague or one of my graduate students who wanted me. My son said, 'I'm sorry, she's playing with me. She can't talk to you,' and hung up on them," Judith said. "And I thought, 'Good for you, Alex!' I didn't say that to him. I was really shocked. I told him he really shouldn't have done that. But wow! How brave of him! But he was also sending me a signal that I was intruding on his time."

Although she silently applauded her son that time, Judith did not, like Indra, believe in remaining silent when kids sent their signals, as it were. Judith, for one, had spoken up on her own behalf. She recounted a time when she was on her way to play tennis one evening for exercise and, frankly, just to blow off steam and have fun. Her son wasn't happy. "He saw me walking out of the house with my racquet and he said, 'Why don't you play during the day, on your time? Don't play on my time.' So it wasn't only the working stuff," Judith said.

"And that, I think, Mika, adds an additional pressure to women, because then you start feeling guilty for what you are doing personally. You want to play tennis or you want to work out, and that's viewed as stealing from the family time. And frankly, you *do* do it stealing from family time."

If I was reading her correctly, it seemed as if Judith did not want to be owned by any one role in her life; she wanted to own it herself. In a way that was where her professional value and her inner value overlaid each other in Venn diagram fashion: "Know yourself—and be true to yourself" could be the phrase that appeared in the merged areas of her professional philosophy and her own as an individual. And that included a healthy amount of personal time.

Personal time? What do I do during my "personal" time? Wait a minute—do I *have* personal time? Is that what I should call it when I take a run while the kids are still in school so I can get it out of the way before they come home? But by the time they get home I usually am already working like a nut. I might as well be out jogging. Sometimes when I'm at home, during my so-called personal time, I'll catch myself juggling three phones at once. I'm on a conference call using my research assistant's phone, on the landline with a family member, and on my own phone, talking with Joe about the show. And I'm actually trying to listen and contribute to three different calls. At the same time. I actually think it's acceptable to do that—that it's even possible to do that. When it comes right down to it, let's be honest: my idea of a personal life drives me crazy.

YOU NEED TO FIND A WAY TO MAKE MONEY

Nely Galán would know what I'm talking about—times about four hundred. Nely knows about being a new mother, being the sole breadwinner and single mother, and being a senior executive in an extremely fast-paced field—all at the same time. Like Indra, she came to a blunt conclusion about the old Women's Movement promise. "Can you have it all—at the same time?" she asked incredulously. "No. . . . I almost missed my personal life completely!"

"I had a child, I got pregnant at thirty-five, had a child at thirty-six, I started a business launching TV channels abroad, so I lived in Mexico City and in Chile, Argentina," Nely explained. "Then when I started running Telemundo and moved back to the United States, I was still traveling every week of the month . . . one week a month in LA, one week in New York, one week in Miami, and one week in Mexico City . . . so until my son was about three, my life was crazy." And with her son's father out of the picture from the start, Nely— just as Indra said she and countless other executive mothers did—had to "co-opt" a team to help raise her son. "My mom came and lived with me for a year, and then my mom was in charge of hiring nannies—and I had nannies 'round the clock because I traveled so much," she explained.

But it wasn't the life she wanted for herself. She could feel her professional value and her inner value—as a "fully and authentically Latina . . . and yet a Latina that can be fully in the mainstream"—begin to wane. After all, she knew, she had always wanted a more typical Latino family life. "I have to say in my most successful moments, at least financially, I was probably the unhappiest because I'm very traditional . . . I really wanted a family, and I wanted a husband, and I wanted all that, and I had to mourn that and let it go," Nely said. "I also didn't think anybody was going to love my kid the right way, so I just sort of decided, 'Okay, I'm just going to be alone. I'm going to sacrifice until my son is eighteen, and I'm going to be a great mom and then see if I can meet someone later in life. I'm alone now and raising this kid, and I'm going to be very successful—and a part of me will be very sad."

Yet it was during those years that Nely rose the highest in her industry's ranks in her career, and she was making a lot of money—so much, she realized, that she could afford to pay nannies at all hours and support her mother's stay during the first years of her son's life. She knew that people who judge working mothers (maybe some of the people in that Pew study) might have said that the fact that she was giving up time with her son to earn increasingly higher levels of income was crass, that a working mother's worth should be judged on her sense of mission. However, Nely knew that she was doing what she had to do. She also knew that that kind of attitude was born of privilege. As the daughter of first-generation Cuban immigrant parents, she said that worrying about whether people are judging you as a mother for earning what they consider to be an unseemly income is itself a "luxury" type of problem.

"It's a very elitist, first-world mentality. Are you going to tell some woman from Cambodia, 'Follow your bliss and the money will come'? That's a lie! The most grounded thing to say is, 'You need to find a way to make money,'" she said frankly. "Money first. If you're in survival, where you need a paycheck, your mission should be: 2 percent of your time and your money should be 98 percent of your time. Until you have enough money that you are done, at whatever level you are done—because everybody is different—then you can spend more time on mission." She illustrated her point with an example of a small business owner in LA. "I went to this nail place, and the lady who runs the place is Vietnamese, and she is the most impressive entrepreneur: the way she buys products and deals with customer service is just so loving and so smart. And she works like a dog," Nely explained. "It warms my heart. And she's not sitting there going, 'Did I follow my bliss?' She's taking care of her family."

For Nely, as she had said earlier, making "enough money that you are done, at whatever level you are done, because everybody is different"—feeling "abundance" and having the wherewithal to support a family—was clearly a very deep part of both her professional value as an entertainment executive and her inner value as a mother, as well as her sense of Latinas' socioeconomic justice and growth. There was no contradiction, no conflict embedded for her in having financial power. What did bother her, she said, was when she saw that her young son, by then a grade-schooler, had grown more attached to his nanny than to her. She also saw that the nanny was smart and had ambition; she needed to grow beyond a job like this.

Nely ran up against an impassable, hard edge. She knew she had to face her sense that if she didn't do something about this situation, it would destroy her inner value, period. Her longing to be the close mother she had always promised herself she would be as well as her commitment to Latina empowerment stood in stark relief. She took stock of her financial situation and concluded that the need to work like a dog wasn't necessary anymore. She had invested wisely, and she owned her own large home in Venice, California, as well as a few small neighboring houses, which she rented out for extra income. She had reached her "enough money" point.

She had suffered to get there, but Nely was now in an extremely powerful place. If she wanted to, she realized, she could use one of her rental properties as an office, work from home, and dial back her hours. She could retain her professional value as a major player in the industry. But she no longer had to be the "always on" entertainment executive, flying constantly between multiple time zones and running on fumes. She could be there for her son when he came home from school. She could help her son's nanny find the work she wanted to do. She could integrate her professional value and inner value as a working mother.

She had cracked the code. She won.

But Nely isn't the only one—not by far. Experience says it. Research says it. There's a major flip side to all this. It turns out that if you're a working mother, you may be giving your children the edge in many areas of their lives. Which is to say that you may have won already.

You just might not know it yet.

CHAPTER SEVEN

"BUILDING A BRAND AROUND IT ALL"

How Successful Careers and Moms Work

*G*lamour editor-in-chief Cindi Leive was due any day with her second child and still happily working full-time at the magazine when she had a flash of exhilaration. "It was a good moment for the magazine, and we won a couple of really big awards," she told me. "And I just remember feeling incredibly lucky and blessed that I could do that and also be nine months pregnant. And it sounds kind of corny, [but] I do look back to that moment, and you know, it just makes me feel incredibly lucky and blessed to be a woman at this moment in time."

Cindi glows with what she calls "provider's pride." She loves her hard-driving job, she loves her family, and she feels great about her life. "Because of how hard I work and how hard I've worked, I'm actually able to give my kids good educations,

177

to have a nice place to live, and to keep our family happy and afloat," she explained. She doesn't feel uncomfortable about being her household's chief breadwinner. "I think if anyone is making a good enough salary to allow the other person to work part-time and spend more time with the kids in this economy, that's a good thing," she said. "That is not anything that anybody should be complaining about." She does feel sad about missing the occasional school event or morning drop-off. But she also loves her job. "And I think also it doesn't mean you're never going to feel guilty. I think any responsible parent feels guilt sometimes on some level: you always want to be with your kids," she reflected. "I think it's fine to feel guilty. It just doesn't mean you have to go and totally change your life."

There you have it: a happy, hard-working mom. They're out there in droves, these happy, hard-working moms. I told you in the last chapter that we were going to get around to the good news in this chapter—and here it is. According to our poll, agreement is consistent across all age groups and household incomes: most breadwinner moms feel pretty good about their lives. Sure, they recognize the complexities of being a working mother and the potential downsides it has on relationships with their spouse and kids. As discussed in the last chapter, poll results and experience certainly show that breadwinner moms are subject to the full spectrum of emotions and parenting potholes that all those remarkable women and I shared about. Perhaps you have them too, which may be one of the reasons you're reading this book.

But still, our survey results show that many of us are not just surviving but prevailing. When asked to characterize how they feel overall about providing for their families, breadwinner mothers are more likely than female breadwinners without children, for example, to say they feel "proud" (50 percent moms versus 32 percent non-moms), "content" (45 percent moms versus 34 percent non-moms), "emotionally secure" (40 percent moms versus 31 percent non-moms), "financially secure" (40 percent moms versus 30 percent non-moms), "empowered" (37 percent moms versus 28 percent non-moms), and "relieved" (27 percent moms versus 19 percent non-moms).

"It has taught me to respect my spouse and kids more for what they do for me at home, as well as outside the home." That is a verbatim quote from one of the breadwinner moms interviewed as part of the survey conducted for this book, responding to the question of how she feels being the primary earner in her family's household. Here is another one, speaking on the same issue: "I think that it teaches my daughter that she can take care of herself, and she does not have to necessarily depend on a man to take financial care of her. That she, too, can have a career and family." This is one I particularly like: "It is all about balance. Both parties in the relationship need to understand the role each plays. Money is not the only asset a person can provide to a family." And as one mother summed it up: "It's a good problem to have, all things considered."

Is it possible to have it all? According to our poll, yes, with 78 percent saying they are successfully able to manage work and family. For women in the northeast United States, the number is even higher: 87 percent of breadwinner moms agree. Consider this chart, pulled from our poll data:

Agree "It is possible to 'have it all'—meaning being able to successfully manage work and family"

	Female bread-winners	Male bread-winners	Bread-winner moms	Bread-winner dads
Strongly agree	27%	38%	26%	37%
Strongly/ somewhat agree	78%	87%	78%	86%
Strongly/ somewhat disagree	22%	13%	22%	14%
Strongly disagree	5%	3%	5%	3%

They're not just having it all either—they're having more. According to a 2013 Pew study, the total family income is highest when the mother, not the father, is the primary provider among married couples with children. In 2011 the median family income was nearly $80,000 for married couples when the wife was the breadwinner—about $2,000 more than it was for couples in which the husband was the primary breadwinner and $10,000 more than for couples in which the spouses' earnings were basically the same, the study reported.

Moreover, most female breadwinners also believe that they're close to their kids and that they're good moms. Fully three in four (74 percent) in our survey agree that their relationship with their children is "as perfect as perfect gets," and six in ten (61 percent) concur with the statement, "I think my children would say that I'm there for them." (By the way, according to a 2013 Pew Research study, mothers give themselves somewhat higher parent approval ratings than do fathers, with 73 percent of mothers saying they are doing an excellent or very good job, compared with 64 percent of fathers. In addition, working mothers give themselves slightly higher ratings than nonworking mothers for the job they are doing as parents; 78 percent and 66 percent respectively. I told you there was good news on the flip side!)

Senator Kirsten Gillibrand (D-NY), junior senator from New York, believes that the main reason she and her husband are doing a pretty good job of raising their two young sons is because her job has built-in flextime, a luxury most of the country's mothers don't have, she pointed out. "I have a lot of flexibility. One of the things I have that the woman who is going to work in this restaurant, the woman who is going to clean it after hours—they don't have flexibility," she said in our meeting at a restaurant in New York City. "They are given hours; they have to work their hours. They might not have sick days. They may not have vacation days. So their challenge of raising their children and doing their jobs is much harder than mine. Mine is a billion times easier because, for example, if I have a sick child, I can bring my kid to work with me. If I need to limit meetings before 9 a.m. so I can take my kids to school, I can do that because I set my own schedule. So yes, I have a juggle that is not dissimilar from a lot of working parents—you know, getting out the door with lunches made, breakfast fed, teeth brushed, soccer uniform in the bag. That's the juggle we all face every morning."

Perhaps in part because of flextime, more than one-third (36 percent) of breadwinner moms report that being the primary earner has had a positive effect on their relationship with their children, compared with half of breadwinner dads (52 percent). Here's the data, pulled from our survey:

Parents say statement applies to them:

	Breadwinner Moms	Breadwinner Dads
I think my children would say that I'm there for them.	61%	63%

Parents strongly/somewhat agree:

	Breadwinner Moms	Breadwinner Dads
My relationship with my children is as perfect as perfect gets—my kids and I are very close. No issues.	74%	80%
I spend as much time as I can with my kids and have gotten flextime or some other flexible work arrangement to do that.	74%	78%
I feel guilty that I can't be there for them like the stay-at-home-parents, and I can see that this alienates me from my children to some degree.	45%	31%

But to me one of the most interesting statistics from our poll is this: those breadwinner moms who *enjoy* being the primary earner overall (57 percent) are more likely than their peers overall to say their career has had a positive impact on their relationship with their children. That is, if you like being the main provider for your family, you're going to feel as though your professional life enhances your children's lives more than a mom who, say, either feels neutral about or doesn't enjoy that role. It seems that if you like what you do, your enthusiasm will spill over into your mother-child connection.

This is what I'm talking about when I say that the closer your professional value overlaps with your inner value, the more you are going to feel more successful in your life as a whole. Those women who are as passionately, joyfully ambitious for their careers as they are for their personal lives to flourish aren't just managing a job and a family successfully— they're loving it, warts and all. Just listen to Claire McCaskill.

HOME HAS BEEN A GROUNDING THING

Senator Claire McCaskill was at work, she said, when the texts started coming in. The messages were seriously challenging her position on two votes in the Senate that had come up that week: one on national security issues, relating to the government's ability to collect information on Americans, and the other on the Keystone Pipeline. The senator had to stop, ground herself, and think carefully about the reasons why she had voted the way that she had before texting back. She had to be on her game. After all, these provoking texts weren't from her typical constituents; they were from her kids.

This is one of the stories Senator McCaskill shared with me during our interview for this book, and I love it. It's a perfect example of how a professional, working woman intertwines her professional value—that of a tough-minded, judicious lawmaker—with the part of her inner value as a mother, thriving on the connection with her children. I learn by listening to the experiences of women like Senator McCaskill because I'll be the first to admit that it has been hard for me to integrate motherhood with my professional life. I've taken my daughters with me on work trips, but they've often ended up feeling alienated because I always have to spend so much time working. Plus, I don't think seeing me in my "always-on mode" is ever an especially welcome experience as far as they're concerned. It's as though I become the "other mother" who reeks of phoniness, manic stress, and probably grandiosity—the one who takes their actual mommy away. I noticed recently that, when I am in crowds, my daughters will scream out, "MIKA!" to get my attention—insinuating that "Mom!" does not work. But the way Senator McCaskill has responded over the years to her children cast a whole different light on how that particular friction with your kids—when your professional life grates against them—can actually bring you closer together.

"I have . . . raised my children to argue with me, and that has been helpful," Senator McCaskill explained to me. "Nothing has been more grounding than coming home and one of your kids calling you out on something you've said or done that they think is phony. They have been a tremendous focus group for me, especially as they've gotten old enough to kind of pay attention to positions I was taking and things and people I was endorsing."

Rather than feel like curling up into a ball and rolling away (as I am wont to do) when her kids take her to task for posturing in an insincere way, she appreciates their feedback, even if it's tough. She relies on her kids' interest and investment in her decisions as a lawmaker—and as their mother—to help root her to what matters. "I can take people being upset with me about votes. It's very hard when my children are pushing back, and I have to be really prepared with my arguments. So home has been a grounding thing for me, particularly once my children got beyond their midteens and started really being thoughtful about things and saying, 'Really, Mom? You're full of it!' "

This was amazing stuff to me. That this high-powered, highly visible mom and her children can have thorny discussions about complex political, emotional, adult topics—with everyone coming away feeling the better and stronger for it—said a lot about the trust, respect, and love undergirding their relationship. Senator McCaskill had not only shown her children that she had great passion for her work and impressed on them her belief in public service; she had also always invited them to engage with her on whatever issues of the day she was mulling over, decisions she had made first as a prosecutor and, later on, as a member of the US Senate. Ergo, her kids, by and large, apparently felt included in her career rather than separated or barred from it.

Senator McCaskill's example proves what the statistics on the women in our poll suggest. If you love what you do as a breadwinner mom, that passion can have a positive effect on your relationships with your children too. And if you value your work, you're more likely to value the positive connec- tions with your children. Says one New York book editor: "One day when I was working, and my daughter wanted me to play with her, I described the novel I was editing. Then I asked her to draw her concept of what the book cover should look like—it's still on my wall. It was just a tiny way to make her feel involved." That's the Venn diagram of overlapping professional value and inner value. That is the kind of success I'm talking about.

But no one is born knowing how to do this dance. To a certain degree you have to watch it first. Senator Gillibrand, for one, found out about how to get what you want from life by watching role models and listening to mentors—from her grandmother, who founded the Albany Democratic Women's Club, to Hillary Clinton. "I had good role models. I had my grandmother who taught me to not be afraid, that public service was a calling—that fighting for what you believe in is something worth your time, that women's voices can really make a difference," she said to me during an interview for this book. "And I learned from my mother that, you know, being different is okay. You don't have to be like everybody else. You can aspire to be a senator. You can aspire to be a congress- woman. You can aspire to take on the Department of Defense if you want. You really can do these things differently if you believe in it." She emphasized, "I also had great mentors. Having the women of the senate like Mary Landrieu giving me guidance; having Hillary Clinton helping me every step of the way when I was deciding whether to run and what it would look like."

Senator McCaskill feels the same way. Rather than taking the credit for modeling for her kids the importance of civic engagement, she credited her own mother for doing the same for her as a kid. "I was just blessed with a mother who spoke out and said what she thought just about all the time, so I had a terrific role model," she said. "My mother used to say things that I found incredibly embarrassing when I was twelve years old. When I was thirty-two years old, I realized how much she was helping me by role modeling, that by taking the safe route and not expressing how you really feel and sublimating what you feel and being so worried about what other people think of you, that you're paralyzed—that you lose out a lot in life." This was a mother who was not afraid to be authentically herself in front of and with her daughter. She wasn't afraid that her daughter wouldn't love her if she spoke out. She had clearly passed on her sense of fearlessness, of confidence to her daughter. And her daughter—while appropriately, tweenagerishly embarrassed—hadn't felt intimidated by her mother but rather had felt a grudging admiration for her that, over time, blossomed into gratitude. Indeed, she had modeled herself on her mother's behavior.

If you didn't have great role models, adopt those of the successful women in this book!

Or try building your own. It's what I'm trying to do too.

Mika Brzezinski

YOU CAN'T LEAD WITHOUT
MAKING SOMEBODY MAD

Hearing about other women's role models makes me reflect on my own background. I was raised with my opinionated statesman father and my artist mother debating current events and politics around the dinner table. All three of us children were expected to dive in at will. My older brothers had never had any problem standing their ground, but I hadn't always been confident enough to put myself out there. In fact, I was reluctant to share any of my opinions for fear of losing face and of being criticized by my outspoken family. Sure, my parents had both modeled for me the importance of being engaged with matters of the world and that, if I could hold my ground, I was an equal. But I hadn't *felt* like an equal; instead, I created a role for myself in order to hide from the family intellectual roughhousing—and potential shaming. Instead of taking a risk and being vocal, I became the masterful party hostess, the dinner table diplomat—in other words, the affable, intelligent news show host.

How does this play out in my relationships with my own kids? Have I been playing out some version of my old family drama around the dinner table, keeping the critics at arm's length by lacquering over my true self and with a candy-glazed persona? Somehow trying to protect my children from my professional self and life, by thinking I *have* to be two people, that my professional value and inner value could not possibly mix at home? When I am trying to pull off my impression of a sis-boom-bah mom bursting with strained bubbly optimism and sugary fretfulness, it's as though I am deliberately trying to hide the part of me that is ambitious, aggressive, high achieving and hard working in a dark closet. Am I my own worst enemy? Am I too chicken or eager to please to open that closet door?

My conversations with all the amazing women in this book have helped open my eyes to the possibility that I—not my work life or family life—am creating my double life. Unconsciously I am pushing my family away from the outspoken, ambitious part of me in a bid to escape their criticism and disapproval—and to fend off their rejection if I try to connect with them in an honest and loving way—by putting up my time-tested party hostess defense.

My fears around not being able to be both a real professional who wants to be taken seriously and a real mother who wants to be loved are valid. Everyone's are. I think we working mothers all have fears around integrating our professional value with our inner value, about unfurling the sum total of our complete personalities in our family's presence. There is something that keeps us from integrating all the passion, drive, and sense of mission we bring to our careers and to our private lives. I have it in my head that my family hates it when I'm working my professional value, that they associate it with a bad acting job, showing off, and an overwhelming work drive. But maybe one of the reasons they hate it is because I almost never bring my Morning Mika self home with me, so it seems like some far-off bigwig boss rather than part of the "real" me.

Or maybe we're a little like Rockefeller Foundation president Judith Rodin, so concerned that family life will erode our professional value that we feel extremely protective of our work lives and personae. Or maybe we're more like PepsiCo CEO Indra Nooyi, self-conscious about our executive power at work when we're at home, so we feel we need to check our crowns at the front door or in our family's presence in any setting. Because we don't want to be accused of throwing our weight around at home, and because we're scared that any parental response will be judged as such, maybe we just keep quiet rather than risk being resented.

But that's not what our family wants either. Maybe they sense that they're not getting all of us, the "real" us, and therefore it causes cognitive dissonance for everyone. Maybe, like Senator McCaskill, we can learn to take the heat as well as the love that our children bring to us—and build the courage to bring our whole selves to the breakfast and dinner table. Or whatever works for you: the Skype session when we're away for work, the back-and-forth texting about whether you're willing to let your daughter have a sleepover that night, talking with our children at the interminable line at the market or in the car on the way to work and school. Whatever our professional bona fides and personae are, we need to integrate them with our personal lives wherever we go. It's a healthy alternative to people-pleasing and feeling like a fake all the time—and distancing ourselves from our personal lives in the process.

This reminds me of something else that Senator McCaskill said during our conversation when the topic turned to the subject of people-pleasing. "All of us have the need to please, but the need to please can become paralyzing," she explained. "In a way a political career is great for that because the longer you do it, the more you realize you can't make everyone happy. In fact, you can't succeed unless you're making some-body mad. You can't lead unless you're making somebody mad. It's *impossible* to lead unless you're making someone mad. . . . I just can't do it and please everyone. And if you do, you just fail, because everybody sees you as the phony waffler that you are, trying to please everyone."

She was, of course, talking about her career on the Hill, but to me she could just as easily have been describing my life as a working mother. As I've described, I'm always feeling incredibly guilty and anxious where my kids are concerned, so when they criticize me, I become the mother of all people-pleasers. And the people I'm trying to dance hardest for are my daughters. It's understandable that my children wouldn't want to interact with that cloying, people-pleasing mom. Maybe they see me for "the phony waffler" that I am, so remorseful about the demands of my job that I'm too afraid to make them mad—by claiming my role either as Mom or in a career that I love, even if it takes me away from them on trips and evenings. Maybe I'm too scared to tell them clearly and honestly that I love them all the time, wherever I am, even though I'm missing important events, and to hear what they would say in response. I'm afraid they won't love me. Or, worse, that they already don't.

But perhaps the real problem is that I am too chicken to trouble the waters by finally acting like the woman I am—a mother, journalist, movement builder, all of it—in front of and with my kids. When, in fact, maybe being authentically myself with them could be the best thing that's ever happened to our relationship: supercharged by ideas, cultural trends, news; excited by the opportunities for women; and being honest about the challenges we all face but don't talk about. These are my challenges and those that my girls will face some day too. Being open with them about who I am, what I have done, what I am proud of, what I regret, what I am still working on. Being myself.

Perhaps this is true for many of us. Maybe the fear and the guilt have to stop. Perhaps we've got to embrace our professional value—to be honest about our power on the job and in the marketplace—and express it to our children and families at home with the same sense of excitement, drive, and confidence we feel when we're at work. Maybe we should let them know that our mother-child bond with them is even stronger than our careers and makes us who we are—at work, home, and in life overall. Perhaps we've got to get over the idea that there's something wrong with being an ambitious mother. Maybe we should stop thinking that we're doing something bad to our children by being passionately engaged in our work. Maybe the "problem" is in our heads.

Or is it? Does a mother's career harm her kids in any objective, calculable, testable way? That is, what exactly have the big brains in the field found about the impact on children of their mothers' working?

A SENSE OF THEIR OWN VALUE

Ever since women started entering the US workplace in (low) double-digit numbers in the 1950s, the American public has been arguing, extremely divisively, about how their mothers' working affects children under eighteen. Even though the labor force has changed dramatically over the years, our society still has a tough time wrapping its collective head around whether Mom being gone during working hours is acceptable for children's development and well-being.

The majority of mothers work for a living (71 percent, according to a 2014 Pew Research report), and the majority of married couples with children in the United States both work for a living (59.1 percent, according to the 2013 Bureau of Labor Statistics), and the percentage of all mothers with children under age eighteen was 69.9 percent in 2013. And as mentioned earlier, only 16 percent of Americans believe that the best thing for children is for mothers to work full-time. According to the Pew report, 60 percent feel that the best way to raise a child is to have at least one parent at home, full time, whereas just 35 percent say it doesn't matter whether parents work or not.

But on what are people basing their beliefs? What's the evidence that mothers working for a living is bad, good, or indifferent for children? How would it even be measured?

Sixty years of studies on the subject has confirmed at least one fact: researchers must test for a great deal more than simply whether the mother works or not if they want accurate results. There are too many other variables in families that shape children's intellectual and social aptitude, most importantly socioeconomic class, whether a father is living at home, whether the mother works full- or part-time, the child's gender, and more. Another consistent finding over the years has been that mothers' working and its effect on kids is largely relative to the cultural norms of the day. For example, a few early studies in the late fifties and sixties found that grade school sons of middle-class working mothers had poorer school performance and lower IQ scores than the sons of stay-at-home mothers. Decades later, in the 1980s, three separate studies revisited the middle-class mother-son relationship to maternal employment and boys' lower performance.

This time two studies out of three didn't find any difference in school performance and IQ between the working and stay-at-home moms, but the third did find lower IQ scores for sons of working middle-class moms. Why the different results? Researchers have a number of hypotheses, among them that in the 1950s and 1960s working mothers were socioeconomic abnormalities, creating a stressful environment for their children at the least on the societal front—if not also financial—because their home lives were different from the majority of their children's peers'. Boys in particular might have been vulnerable because their male self-image might have been impacted by their fathers not providing enough for the family, for example.

But in 1999 a landmark study was led by University of Michigan psychology professor emerita Lois Wladis Hoffman, PhD, and her team. Hoffman published a study whose objective was to retest all previous major findings combined. With a heterogeneous sample size of four hundred families in the urban Midwest, Hoffman's team factored in all the known variables that influence results, but they also tested for new, important contingencies—that maternal employment influenced the mother's sense of well-being, the father's role, and parenting styles, all of which, in turn, influenced the child.

The findings were fascinating. First, the question of whether mothers' jobs hampered boys' performance and cognitive abilities was put to rest. Indeed, the Michigan study reported the opposite, finding that the children of working mothers actually earned higher scores on the three achievement tests for language, reading, and math—across gender, socioeconomic status, and the mother's marital status—even controlling for the mother's education. Indeed, it was one of the strongest findings of the study overall. But they found more.

Previous research had inconsistently found that daughters of working mothers were, for example, more independent and scored higher on socio-emotional adjustment tests but that results for sons was a mixed bag, dependent on their social class and age. The Michigan study now reported that teachers consistently rated employed mothers' daughters, across the board, as being more positively assertive (engaging in class discussions, asking questions when directions weren't clear, at ease in leadership positions), less disruptive, and less likely to act out than daughters of stay-at-home mothers. Moreover, they were more independent, less socially awkward, and had a higher sense of their own value. In both one-parent and two-parent families, working-class working mothers' sons also showed more positive social adjustment when their mothers were employed, although middle-class boys with employed moms acted out more than the sons of stay-at-home mothers. Researchers speculated that these boys might have had less supervision than their working-class peers and were, thus, more likely to engage in comparatively unruly behavior. That is, in working-class homes someone was looking after the kids—a grandparent, an aunt, an uncle—whereas, in middle-class homes adults were either working or simply not around, so those boys were among the tribe of latchkey kids left to their own devices.

Another finding was that sons and daughters of working mothers have less traditional gender-role perspectives. Researchers asked the children whether or not men could do jobs traditionally considered women's work (take care of children, sew, teach school) as well as whether women could do traditionally men's work (e.g., fix a car, climb a mountain, fly a plane). Sons and daughters of working mothers reported that women could do "male" jobs and men could do "female" jobs more than stay-at-home mothers' kids did. What was more, the Michigan study showed that in households in which mothers work, fathers' involvement further significantly boosted their daughters' already higher academic performance and sense of value than those of housewives. Not only did girls have their fathers' support—which is always correlated to girls' higher self-esteem and school achievement—but they also had the example of an independent woman as their maternal role model. Double bonus! It makes me wonder whether husbands of working women are more egalitarian in their thinking and behavior, to boot.

As for the effect of working mothers' well-being on children, the study showed that employed working-class mothers scored lower for depression and higher for happiness and optimism and were more likely than stay-at-home mothers to be firm but fair parents, explaining the reasons for disciplining their children rather than using harsh tactics on one end of the spectrum or allowing children free rein on the other. Interesting, I think, that this is what studies say when researchers observe mothers objectively rather than asking them to self-report. Just think for a minute about what it means that there is such a huge gap between what we think we're doing and what we're actually doing. Again, to me it's fascinating *and* problematic that studies show that working mothers are doing a far better job of raising smart, confident, happy kids than they *think* they are. Moms: let's look at the evidence! We're not doing half-bad here!

To that point, the study also found that working mothers, compared to full-time homemakers, were more likely to report wanting "independence" as a goal for their daughters and were less likely to say that "obedience" or "to be feminine" were important for their daughters to learn. Interestingly, those mothers who said "obedience" and "to be feminine" *were* important were more likely to have cautious girls who tended not to participate in classroom discussions and reported a lower self-esteem, whereas those moms stressing "independence" had daughters who showed the opposite effects.

Again, remember Chapter 6, when I cited our MSNBC poll, which reported that working mothers *felt* more bedraggled overall and guilty about not being there for their kids than the dads did? Objective reporting doesn't confirm it. It just goes to show you that when women are asked to appraise

197

themselves, they judge themselves inordinately harshly. We feel gutted. We feel guilty. We feel we're not doing well by our children, that we're too unavailable to be attentive parents. But research actually shows the opposite: our kids are doing great, by and large. In fact, we may well be giving them a leg up in life because we work for a living. It underscores the aphorism: "Feelings are not facts."

And there's more. In the summer of 2014 a comprehensive study of maternal employment and its impact on infants also debunked earlier research, which had reported poor outcomes for children whose mothers had been employed full-time when they were babies. This study, published in the American Psychological Association's journal, *Developmental Psychology*, found in particular that kindergarteners from lower-income families who were between nine and twenty-four months when their mothers went to work outside the home progress cognitively and socially *as well as or even better than* children with stay-at-home moms.

"Most mothers today return to full-time work soon after childbirth, and they are also likely to remain in the labor market five years later, suggesting the employment decisions soon after childbirth are pivotal to determining mothers' long-term employment," lead study author Caitlin McPherran Lombardi, PhD, of Boston College was reported to have said, according to an APA press release. "Our findings suggest that children from families with limited economic resources may benefit from paid maternal leave policies that have been found to encourage mothers' employment after childbearing."

Therein lies the real problem, the major pothole, for most breadwinner moms. Again it's the battle between reality and perception, a war that takes place in our own minds. The issue is not that children are negatively affected by their mothers working; the issue is a systemic, socioeconomic one. That is, we need to pay working women more—and that's the one thing we should be focusing on instead of feeling guilty, Senator Gillibrand told me in no uncertain terms. "One of the biggest challenges most women face in the work force is they're not paid dollar on the dollar for the same work as men, so the statistics are very troubling. [White] women earn about seventy-eight cents on the dollar. Latinas and African American women earn even less. It means that in eight out of ten families where moms are working, they're not bringing home their fair share, they're not having the money they need to provide for their kids, and for the four out of ten households where the mom is the primary wage earner or sole wage earner, you're really undermining those children's chances of success," she argued. "We're also creating an artificial drag on the economy. If you pay women dollar on the dollar, you could raise the GDP by up to 4 percent. So it's a huge, untapped economic engine," she added.

We're still operating in a sexist, archaic mode, Senator Gillibrand emphasized. "The second thing that's a challenge is [that] our workplace rules are really stuck in the *Mad Men* era. They're stuck in a time when Dad went to work and Mom stayed at home, and that's just not true for most families. Eight out of ten, as I said, moms are working," she said. "So we really need to make sure that the support they need and the flexibility they need through their work life is there. And one of the best ways we can do that is through paid leave."

But there is hope, beyond the Senate and the Hill, that workplace rules will evolve further than *Mad Men*, that they might even be exploded altogether and rewritten. Or perhaps the rules won't even be written down. Maybe the rules will be replaced by a fluidity and flexibility that bends to work and life needs.

By Millennials and entrepreneurs.

CHAPTER EIGHT

ESTABLISHING YOUR BRAND

*How Millennials and Entrepreneurs Can Grow
Their Value from the Ground Up*

Millennials and entrepreneurs. They're both upstarts and outliers. Both famously work "for themselves," driven by a strong set of personal values born of an internal ethos and a passion to be in charge of their destinies. Although published reports say that neither is winning awards for intra-personal likability, both apparently have a high tolerance for change, an appetite to accrue a variety of useful skills, and an impulse to take promising risks. But there's a proving ground. These two types of workers must learn tough lessons in the marketplace to succeed—and even so, the decks seemed stacked against them.

Millennials are the best-educated generation in American history, but they also have the highest jobless rate in recent history. Entrepreneurs have an eight-in-ten failure rate on the market. To be successful, both have to push against discouraging statistics like this, figuring out how to work to market themselves in a way that impresses the people who pay them, meets their own professional and personal goals, and locks down vital contacts at every stage that will help them in the short and long term. Of any two sets of women, knowing and growing their inner value and professional value—and braiding the two together—is essential to their mission in life, personally and at work.

Millennial women and female entrepreneurs are much discussed in the news these days. Ladies, if you fit into either group—or both—you know what I'm talking about. You're both navigating uncharted territory by virtue of your age, your pioneering disposition, and this period of America's socioeconomic history. If both news and academic reports are correct, you are characterized by your drive as independent operators dedicated to living life and to working on your own terms. And although, in general, you are in command of strong traits that people admire and look to as harbingers of the "new" way of working, you are also sitting ducks when it comes to being the target of blame and criticism. Employers and people in the judgment seat love to talk about how entitled, self-absorbed, and lazy you are. Entrepreneurs' failure rate is attributed to impulsivity and a lack of foresight and for not being realistic, prepared, or disciplined enough to handle the prolonged uphill battle.

To the Millennials and entrepreneurs reading this, I say: let's give them nothing to talk about—other than how impressive you are. Other than how handily you turn those stereotypes on their heads. In this chapter women who have done just that are going to tell you how.

MAKE A GREAT FIRST IMPRESSION

My advice to Millennials? Know your audience and be savvy when you interact with these important people. Whether you're a Millennial trying to advance in her career or an entrepreneur trying to drum up investors, these are the people who are going to make it happen for you. Even if you were brought up to appreciate your own inner gifts above all else, you need to learn how to play well with others now.

The truth is that an undue proportion of young women who have crossed my threshold looking for a job—or who have crossed those of my friends' and colleagues'—have not made a great first impression. And I am going to explain why.

I know this sounds harsh, but you need to hear me out on this. You may think you're putting your best foot forward by presenting yourself in your most fabulous attire, but you risk rubbing your potential employer the wrong way. You don't want to make a statement with your outfit when applying for your first or second job. You don't want to be over-dressed and appear as if you don't need the job. You don't want to be underdressed either. It's a fine balance. But here is the key—anyone can afford the perfect outfit, because it should be simple and clean.

Besides, the outfit should not detract from the person. I don't want to be distracted by clothes and accessories rather than paying attention to your credentials. Most employers want what I want: someone scrappy, someone who isn't too proud to do whatever it takes from the get-go to make what we do as successful as possible. The passion to work should be your professional value at the beginning.

A NICE, STRONG LINE

If anyone knows about the subtleties and importance of that sentiment, it's Andre Leon Talley, longtime *Vogue* editor and fashion impresario. From his early days as Andy Warhol's assistant in the mid-1970s to his work with Diana Vreeland and Anna Wintour, Andre has held court at the front row of designers' runways and fashion's inner sanctum. He knows that clothes have the power to say a great deal about a person—and not all of it is positive, particularly when your career is at question. When I talked to him about his experiences as employee and employer over the years and about how clothes make an impact on your professional impression—indeed, on how it is the package in which your professional value is delivered—he had amazing stories and extremely valuable advice to relate. His first piece of advice: dress according to your work culture.

"When I was with Andy [Warhol] I wore a certain kind of look that was very cool and kind of casual. They were wearing blue jeans with those custom made jackets. All the big bosses," he said. "Then when [I went] to *Women's Wear Daily* [I had] another look. . . . I went to my interview at *Women's Wear Daily* in the green shirt that Karl Lagerfeld tossed to me in

May of 1975. In August I got an interview for *Women's Wear Daily*, and I wore the green shirt with a matching muffler because it was fashion, and this was *Women's Wear Daily*," he said. But how did he know when he was putting it on for the interview that the shirt ensemble was going to work for that specific job instead of a position assisting a major artist? "Through my instinct and intuition, through reading and a knowledge of what fashion was. I can't stress [this enough]: Prepare for your interview. Prepare for your subject. You have to be prepared. You may say the wrong thing, but someone will know that what you say comes from somewhere deeply prepared, deep within you. It's entrenched in your own passion."

I asked: Is part of preparing planning on what you are wearing? "Planning what you are wearing, but preparing it appropriately," he said. "Now, I'll tell you another story. I was looking for an assistant [at *Vogue*] and I was interviewing men, girls—girls from different walks of life. The girls were coming in wearing what they thought that I would like: the Calvin Klein with the Gucci bracelets. The right shoe . . . I sit and talk to the girl, and I think, 'She spent more time preparing the right brand, or what she thinks I would like, because it's *Vogue*, than the substance when I am asking her questions!'"

I think the message is not necessarily that it doesn't matter what you wear, but that you shouldn't be so focused on your outfit that it is clear you spent hours fussing with it. Andre agreed. "You are not going to walk in and get a job because you have on the right shoe or the right bag," he said. "Dress with confidence. You could have a sweater and a skirt

or a white shirt or a simple black skirt—I don't suggest you
have a sausage-casing skirt, pencil thin. . . . Just sit down, and
you will just talk with confidence, and you will look the person directly in the eye."

To me the hair and the clothes should not detract from
eye contact. He agreed. "You go in there, and no matter how
much you are trembling, you compose yourself, shake that
person's hand, and you just sit down and look that person in
the eye. And you have to be very, very focused on what you
are doing. . . . Don't say anything false," he continued. "Dan-
gling earrings are strictly forbidden. Dangly, flashing, clank-
ing jewelry. Have a handbag you can put neatly on the floor,
not a status handbag that has a big label. You could have a
little clutch with just a cell phone. . . . You want to see someone looking neat. Neatness. Grooming. Fresh. You might not
even want to have makeup if that's who you are. [You don't]
have to have a makeover. You just have to find your style and
be confident that you are doing the right thing."

Other fantastic advice came from my friend and the
fashion entrepreneur Michelle Smith, founder of Milly. Her
clothing line is one of my favorite labels for projecting my
professional and inner value because its color palettes and
lines are fresh and classic at the same time. Michelle's advice
is great for Millenials and for entrepreneurs going after fund-
ing at big investor meetings—anyone wanting to make a
good first impression on her employer. "You want a potential
employer to see you as a good investment," Michelle wrote
to me in a note. "Keep your look simple and smart, subtly
attractive." Here are some breakout tips Michelle offered up:

- **Hair:** Your hair should be neat, tidy, unfussy. If your hair is more than three inches past the top of your shoulders, pull it back into a sleek ponytail. Long, untidy hair can look overwhelming and unprofessional.

- **Makeup:** You want to look natural and fresh-faced. This means minimal but well-done makeup. Healthy, moisturized skin; a little mascara; a tiny touch of eyeliner; natural lip color. You don't want your makeup to be noticed. Practice a few different options with a professional at a makeup counter until you get it right.

- **Dress:** Invest in a slim, well-cut sheath dress. Do a solid color, not a print. Black or navy is least risky, the best option, but a solid color like dark red is tasteful and could also set you apart from the pack. Length of dress should not be shorter than mid-kneecap. Depending on how formal your chosen field is (legal, banking), a well-cut suit jacket may also be needed. Single-breasted, one to two buttons. A suit jacket is better than a cardigan. Cardigans can read as soft, weak. Jackets give the shoulder a nice, strong line and look more powerful.

- **Shoes:** Always a closed toe. Three- to three-and-a-half-inch heel. Never show your toes. I like the Manolo Blahnik "bb" pointy-toe pump. A great investment shoe as it is classic, never goes out of style. There are some really good, inexpensive copies out there for those on a tighter budget. (Note: Although Michelle and I are tight, here is where we diverge. I would never spend this much money on a pair of shoes; the ones I have were a gift. Just make sure you look for classic and well-made shoes that you can move in with grace.)

- **Jewelry:** Keep it minimal. A tasteful watch, maybe stud earrings. Don't overaccessorize.

THERE'S NO LID ON THE SOUP

Joanna Coles, editor-in-chief of *Cosmopolitan*, had this illuminating piece of advice. "What do Millenials do wrong when they're talking about career? I think they often want a progress report, and they want to talk about their career all the time with their boss, and actually their boss just wants them to do the job," she said to me in her fabulous British accent one morning while we were having a conversation for this book. "So, for example, I have someone who, after two months of working here and doing a perfectly fine job, came to say, could she get on my calendar to talk about her career. . . . So I made time for her, she came in, and she sat down and said, 'I would like to talk about my career,' and I said to her, 'The good news is you still have a job here.' And then I got up and I said, 'Come back in six months' time when you have something meaningful to say.'"

Joanna is hilariously direct, but she is also dead-on. She attributed some of this need to constantly reflect upon and share about one's life and career to a side effect of social media. "I think that they are used to constant affirmation, partly because of the endless 'liking' and 'favorite-ing' on social media—and in real life that doesn't happen. In real life you've got to do a job, and you can't have endless ADD doing your job. Some bits of a job actually require focus and concentration to do well," she added. "I think it's extremely difficult for people to draw boundaries with social media and to come in and to switch it off. And you see everybody working with their phones right next to their desk, and the constant traffic from friends interrupts a more professional relationship that they have at work. It drives me crazy when people e-mail or answer texts in meetings, although I've now noticed I also do it. So I'm as guilty in some ways as other people," she continued. "I think it's hard for people to create boundaries because the phone is with you all the time and you're always on call. I think that's a shame for people because it's good to have boundaries. It's good to know this is your work life and that it gives you space from your parents or from your friends, where you can do something that's about you. And it's good to have a personal life so that you can go home and forget about work if it's not gone particularly well. And, you know, it's almost like a psychological break. I think this relentless 24/7—where we're all connected all the time with each other, and your boss is e-mailing you on a Saturday, and that the boss's e-mail comes in juxtaposed between a Snapchat from a friend and a text from a friend—is a problem."

When we talked about the issue, BBC World News America anchor Katty Kay and coauthor of *The Confidence Code: The Science and Art of Self-Assurance—What Women Should Know* went a step further. She said that, according to her research, she believes social media is creating a generation of young women who feel that they have to be perfect on the surface but who lack inner confidence and drive. "I think this thing of 'the picture' [that one uses in social media] having to be perfect is a big part of [insecurity], and I think social media plays into that. All of these images of women looking perfect. Sending out a Facebook image of yourself in a bikini to see how many likes you get and that instant gratification that comes from social media—which is basically just flattery—doesn't actually build confidence. Confidence comes from things you earn yourself, from overcoming hurdles and working on something. It doesn't come from pressing a 'Like' button on a picture of you in a bikini," she told me as we spoke on the phone about Millennials' need for outside affirmation. (She had just stepped into a cab in Toronto en route to a girls' school to speak about developing confidence!)

"One thing that I say to young women is that if you want to be perfect, you are never going to get there. It's an impossible standard to meet, so stop trying because it is not possible, and it will only eat away at your confidence. If you want to be perfect at everything, then *not* being perfect is going to cause you such psychic damage that you won't take risks, and you won't be prepared to fail. And you know what? Robots are 'perfect'; people aren't."

Katty went on to describe how dangerously pervasive she believes young women's craving for approval is—and how social media doubles down on the problem. "It makes them dependent on other people's perceptions of themselves. It makes them dependent on 'Likes' and comments and other people following them; how many [Facebook] 'Friends' they have and how many followers they have on Instagram. That is not a solid form of confidence; it is a very fragile form of confidence," Katty continued. "Psychologists are very worried that we have brought up a generation of kids with very fragile confidence. They seem very cocky, and you hear employers talking about this all the time. They seem very cocky; they know everything. They [think they] don't have to put the time in and should go straight to the top. But they haven't really been challenged very much. They haven't been allowed to fail and beat hurdles. And when you push them, that cockiness crumbles."

This is extremely troubling to me. What's also concerning, I think, is that I believe that when Millennials look on Facebook, on any social media platform, they see that there are people their age who are changing the world by *creating* these very social media companies, making ridiculous amounts of money and having Wall Street at their beck and call. But what they don't seem to understand is that entrepreneurs like Mark Zuckerberg and the Twitter guys are wildly successful outliers. They're not truly representative of the generation. For every Instagram there are thousands of start-ups that crash and burn before you blink. Not everyone can or even should be wearing a hoodie and launching an IPO.

DON'T TRY TO BEFRIEND YOUR BOSS

Which brings me to another important point for Millennials: do not try to be your boss's friend. Your boss doesn't want to be friends with you. Your boss wants to keep the boundaries intact. And actually those boundaries make your life easier and make your boss feel comfortable with you. When I spoke to Joanna Coles about this, she agreed. "I've become friends with bosses, but I think you always have to respect the line, and I think it's hard for people to do that now," she said. "To me, it's fine to develop friendships and connections. But when you're starting out in your twenties, I think it's important to show that you are focused and that you don't bring everything in your personal life to work with you and let it all hang out." Joanna drove the point home even harder by bringing up another example of yet another Millennial employee who felt that she was overqualified for her job as an assistant—and ended up losing the job because of her attitude.

"The first two or three jobs that you do may not be the most fun you're ever going to have in your life. There will be lots of boring things in them. There will be lots of stuff that you feel is below you—that you *still* need to do and, annoyingly, you *still* need to do it well. And that irritates people!" she said. "I remember we had someone who had come in as an assistant. She had very little experience; she was a very bright girl who wanted to be a writer, and we'd said to her, 'You must write as much as you can, but you have to be able to do this administrative work too, and that's how you get your foot in the door. Maybe your next job will be an assistant editor. But for now, for the next eighteen months, we need you to do this administrative work.' And her excuses for not coming in to work became greater and greater until one day she called up and said, 'My dog ate a pair of my knickers, and I have to take it to the vet.' And I was like, 'And why are we paying you again? I'm sorry: you have to do administrative work. Someone needs to do it. This can't be done by a machine. It needs to be done by a human being. And right now you don't have a big enough skill set for us to put you straight in as an editor. But if you do this and spend 40 percent of your time on the editing work, you'll get there.' But she just couldn't do it."

Joanna agreed with me that this means getting every aspect of the job done right, no matter how menial. (Note to Millennials: getting the coffee is far, far more important in launching your career than you could ever have imagined!) "You have to be able to complete a task, and I think you have to be able to do it with grace. I mean, if someone asks you to go get the coffee, come back with the coffee—with the *right* coffee! I once asked my assistant why he never delegated getting my lunch, and I said, 'For God's sake, have an intern go get my lunch, so you don't have to do it every day.' And he said, 'You don't understand. They can't even go and get your lunch,'" Joanna said. "So to challenge him, I said, 'Right. Let's find an assistant, go, and task them to get me lunch.' And the lunch was soup and a sandwich. When he came back to me, the girl handed me a brown paper bag with some tomato soup and a ham sandwich in it. And the bag fell apart because she hadn't put a lid on it, so the soup had spilled inside the bag. And when we said to her, 'Oh, that's odd, there's no lid on the soup,' she literally turned to [my assistant] and said, 'You didn't tell me to put a lid on the soup.' I mean, it was just ridiculous!"

BLACK EYE MISTO, EXTRA HOT, EXTRA FOAM!

Again, it all comes back to the coffee. That's why I actually say to entry-level women (or entry-level men, for that matter): "Take even getting coffee, getting lunch, running an errand as seriously as if you were dealing with the White House social secretary. These are your tests—these are your chances to prove yourself." I'm glad to know that many of my assistants and the other Millennials I've worked with have taken this to heart. One of them, Daniela Pierre Bravo, had a lot to say about it. I think it's worth sharing here.

"Even before I started at *Morning Joe* I was a huge fan of the show and was excited to meet everyone who sat around the table, especially Mika. Before making my way into television through the NBC Page Program, I had just finished college by way of being a DREAM Act student [which is for those who have grown up undocumented by no fault of their own and have been granted access to higher education through stipulations under Executive Action, thus enabling them apply to obtain work permits]. As such, I gained a certain sense of resilience from facing day-to-day obstacles. I was used to doing the tough job, working around the clock. . . . My thought was that working in television wouldn't compare with the type of challenges I [already] had to struggle to conquer," she wrote.

"Regardless, I was elated at my chance to contribute to *Morning Joe* back then as an NBC Page. One of the most important lessons I learned from Mika came from the first time I met her. I was introduced to her in the midst of getting ready for the show in her dressing room. After telling me she was happy to have me on, she intently asked if I would be the one getting her coffee in the mornings and then followed up with a, 'You better not f—it up!!' This was followed up by laughter around the room. Although partly joking, I was shaken up in a way that allowed me to understand the importance of the tasks ahead with clarity. I understood this wasn't just about coffee. Instead of being intimidated, I saw that as an opportunity to do well and gain Mika's trust. I had to learn and shift my mindset—that although I thought my hardships in the past had prepared me for more than just getting coffee, this simple task wasn't a step back.

"From then on, at the beginning, when one of my tasks of the morning was to get her coffee, I would run to and from Starbucks, understanding her timeframe and the necessity to get it in the earliest window of time possible before the show. The words, 'Black Eye Misto, Extra Hot, Extra Foam!' rang in my head incessantly. When it was still my job to get her coffee, I would check once, check twice, and even a third time with the person behind the counter to make sure it was done right. Even to this day, managing a group of interns who now have that task, I make sure that tune rings the same in their heads every morning: 'Black Eye Misto, Extra Hot, Extra Foam!' I still drill the idea that it is one of the most important tasks of the morning to get done quickly and correctly," she emphasized. "Sure, it's only coffee, but in the end I understood it was more than that. Getting Mika's coffee order right, along with other [seemingly] random demands she requested, had more value than just doing a good job. It allowed me to understand the importance of attention to detail.

"[Carrying out] Mika's demands (which often come with short notice, with a small window of time to get finished, many times during the live show) allowed me to do a better job in my overall role of managing the studio and guests. It allowed me to understand the overall needs of the show better because I gained an acute ear to needs around me. I learned to anticipate those needs, and this helped me to be one step ahead of what was asked of me. This was especially helpful when dealing with four or five requests at the same time while managing the studio during the live show. It stopped being about coffee and quickly became about gaining a greater understanding of attention to detail with the overall production. It became relevant to everything I did, from prepping guests before their appearances to my job with booking and logistics in the afternoon."

Daniela really grasped, in an impressively deep and nuanced way, how important every single component piece is to the whole—making her a tremendous asset now and wherever she will go in her career. "In stressful work environments it's easy to get caught up with finishing bigger-picture matters, but what I've learned is that if you pay attention to the small needs and details early on, you are able to do a better job with the bigger tasks at hand. I have learned to master attention to detail because of Mika, which allowed me to do all my other tasks more effectively and efficiently. It also grounded me and allowed my attitude toward small tasks to rebuke the entitlement stigma most of us Millennials face," she wrote with remarkable insight.

"By working with Mika, especially with the initial interactions I had with her, I have also understood the importance to take cues from those around you, especially your higher-ups. Whatever industry you enter, your first few roles will be to support others. In order to do that, it is imperative to take cues about the needs and preferences of others, because at the end of the day, if you are there in an entry level position, whatever the industry is, you are there to make the jobs of those above you *easier*. That is what gives you added value and helps you excel at your role. What was supposed to be a three-month assignment as an NBC Page eventually led me into a full-time coordinating position for the show—a month and a half into that rotation."

Daniela's message is universal—and she is flourishing as a coordinating producer on the show. She has been given responsibilities that are far beyond her age, and I can honestly say that this is because she took that coffee order as seriously as if her life depended on it.

Another fantastic example is Maria Gronda, *Morning Joe*'s special projects coordinator. Here is her experience in her own words, and then I will add context and advice. "Although it has been over a year since I began my career at NBC, I have never let my guard down. I think it was Mika's celebrity that created an internal triple-check when I would do even the most mundane of tasks, but I will carry that apprehension into every job that I have (whether my future boss has Mika Brzezinski status or not!). If your boss is a celebrity, you can't help but feel replaceable. Through Mika I have recognized the importance of never allowing myself to get comfortable, because comfort can be equated to a lack of drive and respect," she wrote.

"There certainly isn't a blanket rule directing Millennials on how to be the right amount of 'go-getter.' I myself am still trying to figure it all out. The best I can say is: Don't get comfortable, treat your boss like a celebrity, find a way to show your authenticity."

NO TRADE-OFF

I love Maria's message, and I own up to everything in her disclosure. Having said that, I also believe that there is a mixed message that twenty-somethings feel about this kind of advice. After all, I teach women to know their value and to communicate it effectively. So when I tell twenty-somethings to do the grunt work, I know they're thinking, "Well, wait a minute—I thought I was supposed to know my value!" So how do you know when to make that transition from doing all of the irritating work, and doing it really well, to then saying, "Hey, I *am* more, and I *want* more"?

As I mentioned earlier in this book, your boss probably doesn't remember everything you've done, and he or she probably isn't going to come to you. You do need to raise your hand. But how and when should you do that? My opinion is that if you prove yourself the way Daniela or Maria have, you will feel comfortable asking for more. They both did, and they both got more responsibility right away. Again, when I asked

Joanna Coles what she thought, she had a very savvy piece of counsel to offer on the topic.

"It's partly about really doing some research into the environment in which you're working and paying attention to what's going on with other people in the working environment. Look at people who are doing well. What are they doing? Are they doing things you're not doing? If you're ready to have that conversation, and you've got a list of things that you've accomplished—and it might be perfect coffee collection for the last nine months, and you simply can't collect another cup of coffee, then that's fine," she said, wisely.

"But you need to have a list of your achievements, and you need to approach it with real intelligence. Are you being unreasonable? Are you being fair? And if you're being fair, and you feel the environment around you is not rewarding you, then it might be time to move. But I think you *have* to research. How long do people usually stay in this job? Approximately how much do they get paid? If you were working at a different similar place, is it in the same ballpark? You have to find two or three people who are a bit further beyond you, who are a little older, and ask for their advice before you march in [to your boss] and say you need this, this, and this."

As a last bit of counsel, Joanna shared with me—and you—about how important it is for young people just starting out to know how to make and keep contacts—and to have a sense of timing. Part of being able to build and maintain a good professional network is not alienating your superiors *or* your peers. That is, your sense of self-importance, entitlement, and whatever comes across as arrogance can negatively influence your future for years to come.

"I think what's really important is that Millennials begin to understand the value of relationships in the workplace both with your peers, who will eventually be your network that help you get other jobs and tell you stuff and are informed about what's going on in the industry, and also older people," she said. "Actually leaving a place is very important. One person resigned by coming in and going, 'Guess who's the next news editor of *People*'s Style Watch dot com?' And we were like, 'Who?' And she went, 'Me!' And we were just sort of thinking, 'How—what are you saying?' It was a terrible way of resigning."

SEPARATING TWO WORLDS

The relationship point Joanna made was so fascinating and so important. I always tell the Millennials who work for me: "You know what? If you're here with me for more than two or three years, that's your problem, not mine. I want you to do a great job for me. I want you to grow and find your dream through me, and find the next thing. Don't be afraid to tell me about it unless you can create it right here at *Morning Joe*."

For example, I had an assistant for about two years, Sarah Tracey. She came to me just absolutely thrilled because she had gotten recruited for a new job. I'd told her, "Come to events with me. Meet people. Put yourself out there." She did, she impressed everybody, and she got a job at Ralph Lauren. And when she told me, I just said, "That is the best news ever!" And I bet I will see her again; we're still in touch. She is now working with Habitat for Humanity, and we have discussed collaborations. I think there shouldn't be this fear to do a really great job and to navigate through it, and then possibly come back again. Your current boss is tomorrow's contact and potentially your boss in the future—again.

This is what Sarah had to say. "I was working for Mika when she started writing *Knowing Your Value*, and it was incredible to see how many of these lessons applied to me. I was only twenty-three, just a few years into my career, and I heard the message early, which helped shape all of my decisions moving forward. I felt lucky to have landed my dream job right out of college working for a woman who I admired so much. Mika was the one who explained to me that I hadn't won the lottery. I was a hard-working, intelligent young woman, and I deserved to be there," she wrote.

"A few years later, when I had to break the news that I was moving on to a different job, she was the first person to jump up and hug me. Mika was the one who instilled in me the confidence that has been essential to my success. Because of those formative years, I have never had a job I didn't love, and I've never worked for people who didn't value my contributions. With this confidence I also learned quickly to keep my personal life personal. While I expect collaboration and respect from my employers, I also know not to look to them for sympathy or emotional support. Separating those two worlds has made a huge impact on my career.

"Mika helped me see firsthand that as a working woman with a family, you are pulled in so many different directions, and it's just not possible to be perfect or to do everything well. Accepting that I am imperfect and will undoubtedly make mistakes has somehow made me less afraid to try the things that scare me. I feel stronger in my career, but also my relationships," she continued. "It has helped me navigate so many of the difficult situations that young career women find themselves in. I know today that it's okay to ask my boss for more if I know that I deserve it. I have to be my own advocate in all parts of my life. If I work hard, use my talents, and accept that I am doing my best, then I have no problem communicating to my boss that I am a valuable part of the team who deserves the opportunities I've been given.

"Honestly, I was so young when I met Mika and she took me on. I remember exactly where I was when she called and asked if I was up for being her assistant. It led to an experience that completely informed who I am now. Who lets a twenty-one-year-old take control of their schedule, finances, insurance, family stuff? She trusted me completely, and it made me trust myself. There were so many moments where she'd tell me to do something and I'd pause and just stare at her. She was the person who said, 'Of course you can do this, why not?' When I left that job, I was launched into the fashion world, and I knew nothing. I walked into my new office every day and reminded myself of what Mika told me. I can do anything as long as I pay attention, work for it, and stay confident. My boss after Mika would constantly ask me where I cut my teeth. She was blown away."

Having said all this, I also don't want Millennials—or entrepreneurs—to work so hard that they burn out early on in their careers. And that's a genuine concern. Arianna Huffington, media magnate, thought leader, and my friend, had some very helpful thoughts on this. "For far too long, too many women have been operating under the collective delusion that burning out is the necessary price for accomplishment and success," she said. "Recent scientific findings make it clear that this couldn't be less true. Not only is there no trade-off between living a well-rounded life and high performance; performance is actually improved when our lives include time for renewal, wisdom, wonder, and giving," she wrote.

"Here's my advice to young working women: at work and in general, we need to live our lives as women, in our own unique way, not as carbon copies of men. Because our current notion of success, in which we drive ourselves into the ground, if not the grave—in which working to the point of exhaustion and burnout is considered a badge of honor—was put in place by men, in a workplace culture dominated by men. When I was first starting out, I wish I had known that there would be no trade-off between living a well-rounded life and my ability to do good work. I wish I could go back and tell myself, 'Arianna, your performance will actually improve if you can commit to not only working hard, but also unplugging, recharging and renewing yourself.' That would have saved me a lot of unnecessary stress, burnout, and exhaustion."

Senator Claire McCaskill made the point that you've also got to help your boss know what you're capable of. Remember the advice I gave at the beginning of this book, that your boss doesn't remember all that you've done, so raise your hand?

223

Senator McCaskill underlined it. "If more young women would say to their supervisors or their bosses, 'I am happy to do that for you, but I know if you gave me more responsibility in this area, I can really hang the moon. I can really excel.' I think there's a tendency of women to try to do all and be all things so that everything they ever have to do, they think they have to excel at it, rather than taking the liberty of trying to force those people that they work for to know: 'This is really who I am. If you let me do more in this area, it will pay off for you,'" she said.

"When I was in the courtroom, there weren't a lot of women who were trying serious felony cases when I was a young assistant prosecutor. And there was a tendency to shuttle the few women that did it into the kind of cases that were called 'the soft cases.' Welfare fraud, food stamp fraud— things were not violent crime. Not homicide, not rape and sodomy. It was through a mentor that I pushed and said, 'No, I want those kinds of cases.' And rather than say no to one of those files that I was really not prepared to do, I just said, 'I can do it.' I just dove in. And it was, in fact, during one of those trials early in my career that I hit my stride. I said, 'I can do this. I am good at this. There is no reason for me to be worried about the responsibility that I'm going to get. I just need to keep accepting that responsibility and asking for more.'"

But why did Senator McCaskill think young women have such a hard time putting themselves out there—and delivering? "I think there is a dynamic with women, part of this is the nurturing part of us, of security versus power. And when you take risks, one of the things you risk is your security," she mused. "So if you are in a job and you are making good money and you are comfortable, then why rock the boat? Because you're secure. You're bringing home the paycheck. You've got your insurance benefits. Why would you rattle any cages? Because ultimately security is power, but seeing that sometimes is harder for us.

"I make the analogy that sometimes it's like giving money to political candidates. Women will go out and buy a ridiculously expensive purse but will never see themselves writing a check to a candidate because they don't equate helping a candidate who believes what they believe makes them more powerful. Makes their view of the world more powerful. It's the same thing in a career, opting for the safe and secure versus taking the risk and pushing through. And just saying, 'My gosh, I can actually move through this and be in a position where I have power, and I am doing what I love, and I excel.'"

THIS ISN'T KANSAS ANYMORE: EMILY, RASHNA, AND THE WRONG OUTFIT

Emily Cassidy has been my professional manager and executive assistant for over two years now. She works in my home office, which makes her challenges even more precarious because she bridges my life at home, my outside projects like this book, my Know Your Value events, and my job as the cohost of *Morning Joe*. She balances working from her own apartment, my home office, 30 Rock, and coordinating my every move at events around the country. I love the story she decided to tell when we talked about this chapter.

"Over my two-plus years working for Mika we have established a set of rules (all have primarily come from problems we have had to fix). One thing I like about my job is that when something happens, Mika tells me exactly what needs to be corrected; I always know where I stand. One of my favorites of these rules is to always assume other people are going to f—up. I can't tell you how many times this one has been instilled in me. Mika has taught me that it is never acceptable for me to come back and say, 'This didn't get done because so and so didn't do X, Y or Z.' At the end of the day, if she gave me a task, it was on me to get it done, even if someone else dropped the ball," she wrote.

"This means following up with assistants, getting cell phone numbers, getting tracking numbers, following up with phone calls. . . . Never trusting that a job is complete until you are holding the results in your hands. Mika never lets me off the hook because she wants me to think through every possible situation that can go wrong and get in front of it. Getting in the habit of always thinking ten steps ahead has been a priceless career builder."

One of the toughest experiences Emily has had was learning how not to give into people-pleasing. "The hardest lesson I've learned working for Mika and *Morning Joe* is that not everyone needs to like me (and I should assume not everyone does). I am from picturesque Lititz, Pennsylvania, where I grew up in a loving, middle-class family where I was always embraced, welcomed, and celebrated," she wrote. "When I transitioned from my former job as a school teacher in Philadelphia to my current media role in New York City, it was an effort to navigate the many, many changes. I was no longer in the warm embrace of my loving community. I have had to remember that what is most important when I walk into a room representing Mika is that everyone sees me as someone capable and on the clock, working. Whether they like my hair, my dress, or my personality does not matter."

I was so impressed that Emily bravely disclosed her most embarrassing moment to help other Millennials learn from her mistakes. "I learned this lesson on my worst day since starting at *Morning Joe*," she wrote. "I had to travel with Mika and staff her at an event. We were very tight on time, and it was my job to be her front person. I will start with my shoes . . . they were the wrong ones. They were a gift from Mika for a party and were really high, too high for me to move quickly in (and probably even gracefully). Even worse, my outfit was very dressy, and my hair was blown out to look as good as possible. But even though this came from wanting to look impressive, I was dressed for a date, not for work—and Mika let me know in the clearest way later! My problem is, I want people to like me and think positively of me. But that day I was trying too hard, and the decisions I made first thing in the morning set off a chain of events that made for a very bad day on the job because I was not physically able to embrace my role. I was too busy trying to keep up with my outfit."

I did let Emily know that she had botched it later, and truthfully, she has learned much and come far so that she has become a superstar in my life. She puts her heart and soul into everything. Her honesty is so valuable for other Millennials. We had a postmortem about that day, and I was very clear with her about what went wrong and why. I even told her that she had a sense of entitlement, which absolutely shocked her. It was the one thing she pushed back on and took offense over: my calling her "entitled." But we went deeper, and quite frankly, I spent a lot of time talking about this with Emily because she is worth it, and she is someone I want with me for a long time. If she was someone who I did not think was worth it, I would not have spent the time going through and picking apart every aspect of that day. Emily was smart enough to know that and engaged with me in a very real way about how she does her job.

Remember this: when your boss shuts down on you and stops giving you advice, you know you have stepped over the boundaries, and you will never be able to turn back.

I explained that there are different forms of entitlement that can often afflict today's Millennial. Many young people in their first or second jobs expect too much too soon and have been given too much too soon. In the age of social media everything moves fast. Millennials are getting constant feedback, so they often expect that to translate into their professional lives. But this is different from what I meant when I called Emily "entitled." I explained that her loving family and her incredibly supportive friend network was a complete blessing to her growing up as a child, but it actually did not translate well into her professional life. I told her that she had to learn that not everyone in every situation will be as loving and supportive as her family.

And that's where I felt she was entitled. Trust me, there are worse forms of entitlement, and I revere the closeness of

Emily's family. In the real world, though, especially working in New York City, that can give one false confidence. You cannot walk into every situation, assuming everybody is going to embrace you and want you to be there.

In fact, nobody does. Welcome to New York, baby! You have to take your time before you learn your place, especially when meeting new people—and you should assume that everyone you meet is important.

What she now knows is that she needs to be quick, nimble, and able to run down the hall and grab a last-minute script off the printer. She must be in charge, alert, totally on top of it. At the same time, she needs to blend into the background and let me do my thing—always watching for that moment when she will be called upon. She learned a valuable lesson and applied it after our very honest but difficult talk that day.

But where Emily needed to pull back, Rashna needs to push forward. Rashna Shetty has worked at *Morning Joe* for several years as a talent producer and stylist: model looks, the perfect outfit always, and pitch-perfect at every task, scheduling disaster, or event staffing that comes her way. I literally cannot think of anything that Rashna has screwed up, ever. If you ask her to do something, you just know it is going to happen. In fact, her reputation is that she is absolutely perfect. What's wonderful about her is that even when she first came to us in her twenties, she knew exactly how to adapt to any social dynamic at work.

But when it comes to speaking up, I'm the one singing Rashna's praises because I think she is amazing at what she does. My goal is to help Rashna find her voice, advocate for herself, and, ultimately, get her value. At *Morning Joe* we hire winners, and every single one of the Millennial women who work for us are top notch. I nudge them all to know their worth, develop their inner value, and have that fulfilling, authentic life that they want. I'm dedicated to helping Rashna get that.

One thing that Millennials do have going for them is the ability to envision themselves as entrepreneurs. Maggie Murphy spent over two decades in magazines, most recently as editor-in-chief of *Parade*. She spoke about the fact that previous generations of workers didn't feel they had the fluidity that Millennials have. "Structure is helpful for people of my generation who were raised without the idea of being entrepreneurial. We did incredibly well in corporate structures, as you did in CBS, Mika, and as I did at Time Inc. and then at *Parade*. We knew how to lead structural organizations. But starting something new is the biggest leap of all.

"I was sitting next to an entrepreneur who is a college student, and I realized that kids this age are hardwired to start something. Our generation is less wired that way, and that's one of the great challenges in corporate America. For women who have been disrupted in their work lives as I had just been—the organization that you were working for doesn't necessarily exist anymore, so your choices are to completely stop or to start something new. But that is a big leap. So working for a startup is the right job for me at the exact right moment of my career. And that is what made it so amazing."

But in a very real way entrepreneurs, Millennials, and all of us reach a certain point in our careers when our lives run up against hard edges that force us to rethink. That's when we know that our professional value and inner value just aren't in sync anymore—or that we've outgrown one, the other, or both.

That's when it's time to rebrand.

CHAPTER NINE

REBRANDING

When It's Time for a Second Act

Just about everyone needs a rebranding at some point. Life is long. A brand isn't forever. Over the course of your career you may realize that your brand has become tired or isn't working anymore. Or someone new is hired, and his or her brand mirrors yours—but it's bigger and shinier. Or you have an "Aha!" moment and realize you are really good at something (which doesn't happen to be what you're doing for a living now). Or your home life isn't working, and you dial back on your career so that it fits your life better; you work less or work differently—from home a day or two a week, for example, so you can be in better charge of your own schedule. Or you get fed up with the traditional workplace or get laid off and want to start your own business or launch a new career. That's when it's time to start rebranding yourself. In fact, rebranding—reinventing—is a natural part of the career cycle.

Decades ago a career meant working at one company, developing one set of skills, and retiring with a nice pension or package. But let's face it: neither careers nor life has been that way since the 1980s. Today finding a job—and evading layoffs—is harder than ever, which is why people entering the workforce often don't expect to stay at any one job for longer than two to five years. The goal for many Generation Xers and Millennials is to pick up a variety of skills to increase their employability at any given moment. That has also been the goal of two very successful friends of mine, both of whom had been long and well established in their careers when each of their paths made an abrupt U-turn in midlife, forcing each of them not just to figure out how to remap their professional directions, but also to soul-search about who they really were and what they realized they wanted to contribute to people, to society.

My friend, designer, and entrepreneur Michelle Smith debuted her popular clothing label, Milly—a colorful, exuberant collection of women's clothes—at a time of economic prosperity. Then, when the economic recession of the late 2000s hit, she was forced to rethink the entire look and philosophy of the brand. She had to regroup and think about what she really loved doing in order to assert her professional and inner value.

I spoke with her about how she came to terms with knowing that she had to rebrand, inside and out. "From the launch, I exceeded my greatest expectations. When I launched,

I met my yearly business in the first three months. It was amazing, you know—Milly was a success from the start. . . . The business just kept growing and doubling in size each year," she said. "I'd say when we hit the financial crisis—that was probably five, six, seven years into the business—that was the first time I realized, 'Wow, this is not just a piece of cake.' Because up until that point it had been so easy for me. And it was the first time that I was maybe second-guessing myself. . . . The whole market had sort of lost confidence, and no one knew if the clothing they were buying should be the most 'Oh my god!' amazing pieces, or should it be more practical? People won't spend their money on maybe more frivolous pieces. . . . I had to really step back and say, 'What do I really want?' and 'What do I really love?' and only make what I really love. Don't worry about what other people think."

For Michelle this was a turning point. She wasn't just taking a stand on the character of her professional value; she was also listening to the voice that was speaking to her through her sense of inner value and sense of calling. "I want to create pieces that give a woman an emotional reaction and, hopefully, make her feel beautiful and empowered and make her feel fantastic. . . . [But] there was all this confusion swirling around, and it became easy to sort of lose focus on who you are, who I was, and what my strength was. To try to just please other people, please the market. I think I lost track for a few seasons," she said. "And luckily, I just refocused and gained it back. Luckily, I have always owned my own business and been my own boss, so I had the flexibility and the power to make those changes."

235

Michelle's experience brought to mind my own when I refused to read the news on *Morning Joe* that Paris Hilton had just been released from jail. To me it just wasn't news; it was fluffy, gossipy drivel. And even though I was a freelancer on the show at that point, only earning a freelancer's day rate after having been unemployed and depressed during what was for me a very dark period of time, I had a moment of clarity about who I was, my own sense of my professional and inner value. And I ripped up that script, literally, on live television. I didn't care what everybody wanted. I wasn't going to read something that I did not consider real news on the air. It wasn't in me anymore to people-please on that scale. So I simply refused to do it. I could have been fired on the spot—and almost was. But that was also a moment in which everything came together. Joe loved it, and our viewers loved it. E-mails, Tweets, messages of all kinds came in from viewers who, like me, were sick of celebrity gossip being passed off as news. They applauded my move. It was my defining moment, as it turned out. It catapulted my professional value and my television career.

Michelle had a similar moment of clarity. "There were several seasons where I was so confused during . . . about 2009 . . . from a fashion point of view, when I launched, what I was doing was very 'in,' in 2001. It was coming out of the minimalist nineties where everything was very black and sort of very technical and serious. And what I was doing was very feminine and bright and colorful, and stores like Barney's thought that was revolutionary—that I was doing colors and feminine florals. They were snapping up my collections like, 'Oh my god, how avant-garde!' It was funny, right? Because it was so different at the time," she said. "But then by 2009, fashion had shifted. There was the whole shift to a very tough, aggressive sort of 'urban protection' look—you know, very androgynous. Leather, black, tough, biker. It shifted fashion across the board. And it really had nothing to do with where my heart and soul was . . . [but] I was really dependent on the large luxury retailers buying my collection. That's what they wanted, so I had to bend a little bit. But I just feel like I sold my soul to the devil a bit for a few years."

Once she came out of that period Michelle had a firmer sense of who she was—and, therefore, what her business was. " 'Perfectly imperfect' is kind of my life. I'm a mother, I have my own business, and I'm working hard, but I'm not perfect. My Instagram is not full of perfectly staged photos with professional makeup and lighting . . . it's very off the cuff. It's real life. In the moment. I'm not afraid to show that to my customer. I think my customer is a lot like me, and we are all in the same boat together." She is now rebranding Milly as not only a clothing label but a lifestyle brand—and Michelle is sharing her experience with our audiences at my next Know Your Value conference.

A BRAND ISN'T FOREVER

I spoke with Maggie Murphy on *Morning Joe* in September 2014 and again later for this book. Maggie is a great example of someone who has rebranded after working for over two decades in magazines, most recently as editor-in-chief of *Parade* magazine.

"When *Parade* was sold to a new company last October, the entire staff was let go. That's when I realized that I hadn't actually looked for a job in twenty-six years," Maggie continued. "I had moved from one position to another, from *Us* to *Entertainment Weekly* to *InStyle* to *Life* to *People* to *Parade*. A lot of people encouraged me to take time off, to think and reflect. But that didn't sit with my DNA or my life situation. I have a husband, a child, a disabled sibling, and an elderly mother who are dependent upon me. I have worked since I was sixteen, and working is who I am. It's the Mary Richards in me. I really enjoy tossing my beret in the air and moving toward something.

"But publishing is in a disruptive moment," she said. "Things that were venerable truths are no longer true. And the thing that intimidated me was the transition: Can I find a place in what's now a very different business? There was the fact that I wasn't a kid anymore. In fact, the kids I knew were suddenly getting the really big jobs. I'll admit there was this feeling of, 'Oh my god, if they have that job—then what jobs are left?' I don't know if men feel this way, but I believe that many women worry about being displaced at a certain age.

"After the news of the sale was announced, the staff basically got together and started sharing résumé ideas and leads. They knew how to take care of themselves: 'Okay, here's how we're going to do this, and here's how we're going to act.' That's when I realized what I had taught them being their editor-in-chief. That's when I recognized what my brand is; it is empowering people. I do that well, so I needed to launch that skill in a new place. I know people like working for me, and I like working for people. So I just had to figure out how to translate that into a paycheck with health insurance!

"What I also tried to do is understand what isn't on a résumé that might help me better pitch myself to a new employer. One of the things about me that you don't get from a résumé is the fact that I can talk to anybody. I can talk to the president of the United States for a *Parade* interview. I can talk to Mika Brzezinski on national television. And I can talk to the woman at the cash register at Walmart. I had never completely realized that this is my gift—that I can go to a playground or I can go to the White House, and I can start a conversation with somebody. So I tried to not think of my next job solely by my last job's specific parameters: 'I work at a magazine.' Instead, what can I do with that talent of being able to converse with people, and where does that skill belong now? It may not belong in the traditional universe that I'm used to. Maybe it belongs somewhere else.

"I started meeting folks, using my reporting skills, and figuring out what the opportunities could be. And that's my first piece of advice to people who find themselves in an industry disrupted by change like mine has been. Decide that you wish to be part of that change—and of course you have to make a commitment both emotionally and financially—and then take steps toward achieving that. I know it can be demoralizing to fill out your hundredth job form—and you realize just how messed up the entire HR system is—but knowing that I was moving toward a next step kept me pushing on.

"I also tried to put my career in perspective for someone looking at my résumé. Working for Time Inc. helped me to be

239

somebody," Maggie stated. "At *Parade* I learned to lead. I loved being editor-in-chief, but I decided I definitely wanted my next job to be about building something. And that's what I am doing right now. I joined Some Spider in January. It's a digital startup, and it's transitioning to be a multibrand lifestyle site; our site includes themid.com. I am the oldest person in the room—and the office is a big room; it's a kick in itself to be working in an open space again after occupying the corner office for so long.The topics are the ones that matter to me and to anyone in the middle of life: your family, your friendships, balancing work and life, and, of course, how pop culture reflects and defines it all.

"How I got the job gets to my second piece of advice. Despite all the wonderful tools out there to help you job hunt, it still comes down to contacts, and it isn't always the ones you've had for decades. A fellow by the name of Bill Murphy (no relation) responded to my note to him after I read about Vinit Bharara, the owner of Some Spider, in the *New York Times*. Bill helped bring me into the company last fall when I reached out to him. Those casual connections are sometimes the ones that really make things click.

"Along these lines, anyone who feels they may soon be downsized should start thinking about their peer groups differently. I have many wonderful peers and C-suite men and women in my corner. So many have done terrific things in terms of introductions and support. But here's the truly amazing thing that I discovered these last few months: the people I once mentored now truly mentor me. These wonderful young women and men who were so smart and talented that

I couldn't help but befriend them have turned out to be the most inspiring folks to talk to. They gave me great advice. They helped me understand the new work world in a different way. They tweaked my pitch and helped me understand how to position myself," she added.

"In fact, once I get settled in this job, another displaced editor and I hope to start a new kind of media group. It will be formed around the idea of getting all these terrific peers and all these bright younger folks together to help foster a different kind of mentoring. I think that in an industry as disrupted as publishing is right now, you have to both value your history and experience, but also work hard to know what you don't know. Add some cocktails, and who knows what we might discover and create!" Maggie said.

"In terms of my job search, two moments really stand out. During a low week—when two back-to-back HR conversations went nowhere—my friend Sandy, who has gone through her share of job mergers and acquisitions, told me something a friend told her: 'Maggie, just remember, there's a job out there looking for *you*.' It's an old saw, but it really made me feel more in control."

Maggie smiled. "The other insight came as I walked my daughter Maeve home from school one chilly November day. As a working mom, I didn't do a lot of school pickup, so I thought it would be great. And it was. We stopped at the new crepe shop, shared confidences about her dad. It was just nice to see her in the afternoon on a weekday. But I must admit that as the days grew shorter and it seemed like I was spinning my wheels through job search engines, I longed for the routine of my old work day and being around people whose problems I could solve.

"This dovetailed with the fact that as the school year progressed, I found my daughter's post-bus conversation a bit of a bummer. When I asked her how her day was one afternoon, I got slammed with, 'There's so much homework.' How she had hated lunch that day. And French was still making her miserable. After feeling a bit lost in my own skin in those weeks, the boss in me came back to life. I decided it was time to manage the situation," Maggie recalled. "I told her that from then on, I would give her ten minutes to vent about all that was wrong at school that day, but then she was going to have to tell me one thing she was going to do about it. I might be out of work, but I was capable of creating a positive working environment. I am not sure how this will all come out in Maeve's version many years down the line, but I do know that staying positive, being around positive people, asking people to find solutions, and asking for help and encouragement at every turn is probably the best thing you can do for yourself. It's also the best thing you can do for anyone you know [who] is in the midst of a transition."

I had a similar rebranding journey. The year before kismet introduced me to Joe Scarborough and his morning news show at MSNBC, I was floundering at work and at home. Having been fired from CBS because, I now believe, I hadn't grasped my true professional value and, thus, hadn't made it clear to the network muckety-mucks how best to use me as an on-air reporter, I was out there hustling, but with no results.

Now I can see why. If psychoanalysts had read my résumé, they probably would have interpreted my professional life as that of a workaholic: willing to put in any amount of time and energy into whatever job you threw at me but overeager and unfocused. Now I was at home full-time, for the first time in my life a stay-at-home mom. And I was jittery and distracted in that role. In hindsight I was suffering a major identity crisis. I had been in TV news ever since I was an intern at age fifteen, and my whole self-concept was inextricably linked to working in the field 24/7. But I had no work now, and no one was hiring me. I was between two worlds, and at age forty, I didn't know who I was.

With nothing else to lose, I ended up taking a practically entry-level job reading news during the daytime at a puny freelance wage at MSNBC, where virtually no one remembered my longtime career in TV news. But unexpectedly, being just another face, a worker among workers, gave me the courage to just be myself on air: down to earth, self-assured, curious, direct. That personality worked well with Joe Scarborough and, subsequently, the producers of *Morning Joe*. Within the next year I became cohost of one of the most innovative and exciting news shows on television. I had successfully rebranded myself.

It may seem a challenge to rebrand yourself, but consider the story of Bonny Warner Simi, who has done it four times. The three-time Olympian, TV broadcaster, airline pilot, and Fortune 500 executive says, "Life is full of chapters, and to keep passionate and excited about work, it makes sense to turn the pages on a new chapter every dozen years or so." Although Bonny has had some overlap in her "chapters" (which, she says, is one of the keys of success), she has indeed changed chapters and rebranded every ten to twelve years.

As a child growing up in southern California, Bonny watched the Olympics on TV and came home one day from school to tell her mother that she wanted to be an Olympian and also to work for ABC-TV (the network that covered the Olympics at that time). She also made a list of a few other things she wanted to accomplish, including going to a good college and learning to fly. Any one of these would be a big dream for a fourteen-year-old kid who lived with her single mother and two brothers, with little means in a small mountain village.

In high school she competed in a full menu of sports, though never at an "Olympic level," but the sport of field hockey did get her a full scholarship to Stanford University, her dream school. While there she won an essay contest to be a torchbearer for the 1980 Olympics in Lake Placid, and that is where she tried the sport of luge.

Throwing herself fully into competitive luge (while juggling college and field hockey), she did earn a spot on the 1984 Olympic team, and this is where most people would say "Success!"—but not Bonny. She remembered her childhood dream of becoming an ABC-TV reporter. "When the local ABC-TV station in San Francisco came to Stanford to do a story on the Olympics, I convinced them that perhaps they needed an 'insider's point of view' by having an athlete help with stories from the Olympics." Bonny was finishing her degree in broadcast journalism, so the job offer for a freelance job (and then, later, a full-time job) as writer-reporter-producer for KGO-TV (ABC) was not only in line with her dreams but also her qualifications and education. Bonny continued at KGO and then went on to cover several Olympics for ABC, CBS, and NBC as each of the networks earned the rights for the Olympics. This was Bonny's "second chapter," rebranding from athlete to TV commentator. Most would be happy with this and say "Success!"—but not Bonny.

She also had a dream of learning to fly, so after college and several years on the job, she earned enough to get her wings and quickly fell in love with aviation. She starting teaching flying and later picked up odd jobs flying corporate aircraft to build experience. After many years of juggling both professions, she made the decision to go full-time as an airline pilot. "I walked into my boss's office at KGO-TV and told him I was accepting a job at United Airlines. He told me I was crazy, because nobody gives up a reporter job in one of the top markets in the country. I told him I had to follow my passion, and he understood."

Bonny spent thirteen years at United, flying both domestically and internationally while also continuing her Olympic quest. She competed in her third Olympics in luge and transitioned to the sport of bobsled—rebranded herself as an athlete. She was ranked third in the world and was alternate to the 2002 Olympics (her fourth) and then retired from sport so she could do the commentary for NBC for the Salt Lake City Olympics.

By 2003 she was a Boeing 737 captain at United and was fairly senior, which gave her a good schedule and allowed her to raise a family. At this point most would say "Success!"—but not Bonny; she never lets moss grow under her feet. "I still enjoyed flying, but I wanted to do more. I became very interested in the business side of airlines and took some time to get degrees in HR, business, and engineering. At that point Jet-Blue Airways was just getting started, and I was very intrigued by their customer- and employee-friendly business model, so I decided to make a big career change—and leave United for JetBlue. When I told the United chief pilot, he told me I was crazy because nobody gives up a seniority number at a major airline to start over somewhere else. But I knew I wanted to follow my passion."

This was Bonny's fourth big career move/rebranding. She started at JetBlue as a junior pilot (first officer) and later became a captain. However, what intrigued her was the business side—and she spent several years in various departments across the company and is now the VP of talent. In her current role she oversees all the hiring for the Fortune 500 company as well as leadership development, performance management, and other human resources functions. She also maintains her currency as an airline captain and flies frequently. Although she no longer competes at the Olympic level in sports, her sixteen-year-old daughter is now a member of the Junior National Luge team.

From Olympian to TV commentator to airline pilot to Fortune 500 executive, Bonny has rebranded herself many times—(and may not be finished yet). What advice does she have for others considering major career rebranding? "Above all, follow your passions. Find a way to get paid for doing what you love; that way you'll never 'work' a day in your life. If you are just punching a clock, then every day is work—and it is time to explore other options. Never be afraid to take a big career leap, even if others think you are crazy. One way to reduce the riskiness of a career change is to do both at once— both your old role and the new one—until you're comfortable with following your heart. Passion is contagious, and others will believe in you if you believe in yourself."

TURNING IT AROUND IN YOUR OWN LIFE

I've known Diane Smith for years. She was the colleague of my husband's whom I mentioned earlier—the woman I had asked to drive me to the hospital when Jim was out of town and I went into labor with my second child. Diane was basically like my sister during that childbirth—holding my hand, soothing me through painful contractions, and being right there for the delivery of my beautiful daughter Carlie. After that seismic bonding experience, Diane and I have been dear friends ever since.

A career Connecticut TV reporter, Diane had for years been the brain and voice of a regular and much-beloved segment called *Positively Connecticut*. With her characteristic vigor, smarts, and enthusiasm, Diane reported on uplifting stories, a welcome break from the often depressing or violent pieces local news stations are known for running. She was famous throughout the state, viewers loved her, and, just like her show, everything about her radiated "upbeat." Except for

247

one thing: she struggled with obesity, a condition that had gotten worse over the years. She never talked about it; she was in complete denial. Confronting negativity—even if it was the blunt truth—did not mesh with the brand identity Diane had built over the years.

But through all her trademark charm, I could see that her inner demons tormented her. Moreover, after expanding *Positively Connecticut* into books, a half-hour TV program, and a radio show, the brand needed a reboot. It was time for Diane to look at her life from the inside out. For Diane, it seemed like everything was leading to a dead end. She was ripe for a rebranding and for rediscovering her amazing value.

I said to her, "Diane, it's time for you to rebrand. What's your new brand going to be?" She looked at me blankly. I told her that she had been in an unending battle with her weight but that she needed to start a journey and fight it, once and for all.

I believed in Diane as a professional, and I cared about her as a friend—and that included her health. I said, "Look, here's the deal. Obesity is a huge problem in this country. It's not just you—it's all kinds of people. And it's getting worse and worse. It's going to impact our economy and our health care system. So here's what we're going to do. You're going to make yourself over into a healthier person, and that's going to be your new brand. You're going to talk about obesity, about public policy. You're going to become an expert on what's happening in this country that's making us fat *and* tell a compelling story about turning it around in your own life."

Diane and I collaborated on my book, *Obsessed: America's Food Addiction—and My Own*. By the end of it we had learned more about ourselves and each other than we'd ever expected. It was painful—confronting our own psychic bugaboos was taxing at every step, and the work was exhausting. But our final product was fresh and honest, and it resonated with readers.

To me there is always an opportunity to rebrand, and Diane took the ball and ran with it. She looks and feels amazing. While we are both still employed in TV news reporting, our brand identities are now richer and more multifaceted than ever.

Our brand identities shifted because we got personal. We had the guts to be vulnerable and connect. We investigated our own inner lives. We laid bare our personal stories as they related to the topics we were covering as journalists. We inserted ourselves into the story of America's obsession with food. We became real faces that readers could attach to the problems and controversies of the day. We chronicled our stumbles, our wipeouts, our day-to-day battles, and our victories, no matter how small.

In writing the book and following its publication, Diane and I each had our own separate rebranding journey, but to both of us, the experience was wonderfully and oddly freeing. For the first time in our lives each of us felt as though her public self and the deepest part of the mind's secret psyche were finally—in midlife, no less—merging into one whole person.

You may be wondering: How do I get a rebrand like that? The short answer is: if you duplicated our rebrand, it wouldn't really be yours. Instead, look inside yourself. The rebranding process begins with no small degree of soul-searching. What do I love to do? Where do I want to go with it? How does what I've accomplished so far help to position my rebrand? Most importantly, ask yourself if you feel at peace—not if you are "happy." To me, aiming for "happiness" is like shooting at a moving target: as soon as you think you've got it locked down, it shifts. Finding peace is the real accomplishment.

I had a moment of peace when I took on my role at *Morning Joe*. When nobody else knew it, I could tell that the show was going to be great. It was the first interesting show that I had ever been on. I felt a sense of professional serenity: this was the job I wanted, there was no other job that would be better for me, and I could grow other brands from it.

But the moment when I finally felt personal peace was during the process of writing this book. Hearing from other women about their challenges at home and their stressful careers. Being able to come to terms with and share my own. Growing my value has finally made me feel like I can enjoy the moment. No more faking and pushing round knobs into square holes. I now relish moments with my family and miss work when I need to, cancel a meeting if I am too tired, and enjoy truly connecting with my very patient family. I have arrived—and I love my jobs, all of them . . . at home and on the road.

This is exactly the route that former Clinton White House press secretary Dee Dee Myers took when she finally left Washington and a lifetime career in political consulting and communications. She decided to enlarge her career and family life on the other side of the country in an entirely new business. Dee Dee had just moved to Los Angeles to start her communications career in the entertainment industry at Warner Bros. when I talked with her about what it was like to shift gears—and coasts—in midlife.

ONE OF THE ADVANTAGES OF GETTING OLDER

If you're old enough to have voted in 1992, you know all about Dee Dee Myers. The first woman and the second-youngest White House press secretary in history, Dee Dee was just thirty-one years old when then-President-elect Bill Clinton tapped her to head up that vaunted office. When I look at pictures of her back then—with her short, coiffed hair and gorgeous Brooke Shields eyebrows—it makes me chuckle with delight, remembering how implausibly young and superbly competent she was in that groundbreaking role.

For years after her tenure at the White House Dee Dee was a mainstay on TV news programs as a political analyst (including with us on *Morning Joe*) as well as serving as a consultant to Aaron Sorkin on the smart, addictive, award-winning television series *The West Wing*. She also headed up her own Washington consulting firm, Dee Dee Myers, Inc. She went on to join the Glover Park Group, a Washington communications and lobbying power center, as managing director of strategic communications. But after a more than twenty-year career navigating the relentless high wire of Washington politics, Dee Dee decided it was time for a rebranding. She had lived, breathed, eaten, slept, spoken—done—Washington. She had worked a Washington schedule. Now in her early fifties, with a fourteen- and eleven-year-old and a husband of eighteen years, she wanted to try her hand at what Beltway insiders sometimes call "the other Washington": that other one-company town, Hollywood.

"At fifty-two, you don't really have the amount of opportunities to look at your skill set and say, 'What do I want to do?' and 'How can I get there?'" she said candidly. "I sort of had my antenna up because I was open to something. I thought, 'I don't have a tremendous amount of time if I'm going to do something that's going to be really different.' I could have gone and done something in Washington, and that would have been a big change, but [this was] something really different."

Before I asked her about her new job, I was keen to hear exactly why and how she had put her "antenna up." What had driven her to jump into the reinvention pool when she was a Washington mainstay? "I think you have to be open to possibilities. It doesn't mean you have to take everything that comes along, but you have to be open to it. You have to be willing to try it on. You have to be kind of like, 'I could do that, I could do that, I could do that,' as you look around and believe that you *could* do that. Because I feel that at fifty, you know what your skill set is. It's one of the advantages of getting older, [though] there are plenty of disadvantages," she said frankly.

In fact, it was her sense that her particular know-how was becoming irrelevant that had compelled her to join the Glover Park Group in 2010. "I feel like I made a very conscious decision to come to Glover Park because I had been working for myself for so long. I thought, 'There are things that are happening that I don't know about, there are skills out there in new media, in social media' . . . and I wanted to go into a different environment where I knew I could apply my skill set but that I was going to learn stuff I didn't know. So that was a very conscious decision but always with the expectation that it was a step to something else. I loved Glover Park, so I wasn't looking to leave, exactly. But I didn't think that was the final destination. I didn't think that I would be there fifteen years."

Listening to Dee Dee talk, it struck me that she had incredible self-knowledge. And that self-knowledge had emerged as an invaluable tool in carving out a rebranded life for herself: understanding, for example, that she's the kind of person who is going to want to widen her perspective and career down the road, that she's someone who sees herself working past sixty-five. This is key, in my opinion. If you have that kind of insight and foresight—even if you don't know exactly where you're going ultimately—you nonetheless have a solid sense of your basic direction. That is, you know that you're in store for a rebranding, even if you have no idea how your career and life might change in specific terms. This is hugely important. Because although that personal intelligence on its own might not pack enough momentum for a big push in your life, it certainly staves off inertia and keeps you alert to rebranding opportunities—and you're positioned to act when they present themselves.

That kind of insight and foresight was clearly a major reason Dee Dee had kept those antennae up, so I asked her to describe to me how the job had crossed her path. "I really thought that I was going to get Warner Bros. as a client; this is how I got into conversation with them. I knew they were looking for a communications person or they were getting ready to. . . . I met [the new CEO], and all of a sudden I felt like the Dick Cheney of Warner Bros.: I was going to help them find the right person, and I ended up taking the job myself!" she said. "But it wasn't obvious . . . [because] although I worked in media, I never worked in the entertainment business, and I have never worked for a big company. And I said that to my now-boss . . . and he said, 'No, no, no, I want diversity'—and he's Japanese American. He says, 'not like me, although that's important too. I want people who have all kinds of different backgrounds sitting around the table. I want all those different perspectives.' Which was a very compelling argument for me, both as, 'Maybe I could fit in here,' and also, 'That's the kind of guy I want to work for.'"

As I thought about it more, I realized that Dee Dee's rebranding journey was amazing for a number of reasons, not the least of which was that everything on her résumé that she worried was a drawback was actually seen as valuable. Dee Dee's age, her professional experience, and even her seemingly ill-matched background all turned out to be advantages when the right rebranding moment arrived.

This confirmed something that I firmly believe. If you know how to extract the fundamental learning from your past work experience and you can see how it ties into your brand now, any part of your background—even those parts that you perceive as unimportant, detrimental, or to have taken place so long ago so as not to matter anymore—can and will attract the new job, venture, or change that you were waiting for. Even if you didn't know that you were waiting for it.

Believe me, there's nothing magic here. It's all about how you see yourself and your place in your field and in the world. If you're confident and assertive about your background and you do in fact have the chops to do those jobs that are potentially of interest to you, you're already maneuvering yourself into a good spot. You project accomplishment. You radiate success. You embody your professional and inner value. You're already in the game.

In Dee Dee's case her background at the White House was still relevant to her professional value, even more than twenty years old. "Coming out of the White House, I was young when I went in, and I was young when I went out. I think that was part of my brand, and I think it wasn't necessarily the strongest part. But I think you go to the White House . . . and you become a veteran, your experience is so intense. So you're young, on the one hand. On the other hand, you've survived the crucible of the inner sanctum of American politics," she said philosophically. "No one looks at me and thinks 'young' anymore, but there are a lot of benefits on the other side of that. I think because I've been around for such a long time, that gives me a certain amount of experience and calm in a crisis—and I think one of the things about going through the White House in your early thirties is that you really learn how to distinguish between something that is a crisis and something that is important but not a crisis. And that lesson has been very valuable to me in many settings, [including] the one where I am now, where we have important problems and urgent challenges, but we rarely have a full-blown crisis—no one is going to die."

Although she was confident that her brand value could morph into a new career, Dee Dee was also intent on protecting her inner value as a mom first and foremost. Indeed, knowing that family time would not be at risk in Warner Bros.'s work culture was a major reason she took the job there. "I work hard, but I also have boundaries around it. . . . People [at Warner Bros.] have lives, which is another reason I was willing to take a risk on this. I talked to people, and they were like, 'People work hard when they have to be there, and when they don't have to be there—and know the difference—they go home to their families, and that's something that is valued and respected by colleagues,'" she emphasized.

She also talked at length about how important it was that the company had been flexible in allowing her to move after her children's school was out for the summer as well as how essential it was that they find just the right fit in new schools for their kids to ease the transition of moving coasts. It was clear that Dee Dee's inner value, derived from time with her family and at home, was every bit as important to her as making this bold rebranding move. "You know, we have dinner [as a family] every night . . . I really limit the times I go out. I have a little more of that here; there are movie premieres you have to go to, and it's important to show up. But if it's optional, even if it's something I want to go to, I don't go," she said. "My daughter . . . is in the school musical and has rehearsal until six o'clock, so she gets home a little before me. But I've got to get home before 6:30 p.m. when I can."

I love that because Dee Dee knew how she had already established herself in her career, she was able to grow when the time came. I also find her path and outlook very grounded. Even though she didn't know exactly what a rebrand would look like, she knew that eventually she would want a change and that she would recognize the right move when she saw it.

But the path to rebranding doesn't unfold in such an indirect and thoughtful way for everyone. Not at all. For some the need to rebrand comes on suddenly and all at once. It seems to come out of the blue, when it's in fact the outcome of living through a period—sometimes a long period—of unhappiness or upheaval. Instead of rebranding in the form of a job hunt, such experiences can be more like heightened moments in which you feel called to do something you realize you have always wanted to do but hadn't known it before. I have had that experience. Twice. So has television executive impresario Nely Galán—times a thousand.

THE LIFE I WANT

When Nely started working from home because she saw that her son was growing more attached to his nanny than he was to her, she had another revelation—again, triggered by her son. "My eight-year-old son said to me, 'Mom, why do I need to go to college? You never really finished college, and you've done really well.' And I thought, 'Oh my God, that is a thorn in my heart!' I did get into TV early in my career, and I dropped out of college, but I am a very studious person and I didn't want my kid to think that [not graduating] was okay," she said. "So my husband, who at that time was in our life by that point, said . . . 'If you were going to die in a year, what would be on your bucket list?' And I said, 'I would go back to school and I'd get a doctorate.' And he goes, 'Then you should do it.'"

So she did. With her life's accomplishments as the wind at her back, Nely took a sabbatical from her career at the end of 2008, went back to school, and earned a master's and doctorate in clinical psychology in just four years by attending courses all year round. Specializing in family therapy, she worked in a free clinic in LA as a therapist treating gang families. "It's the single-greatest thing I've ever done. I feel like it completely changed my life for the better, and it made me walk through my fears of thinking that if I go away, I'll never work again. Which is ridiculous. It helped me to close a lot of issues in my own life and really deal with a lot of issues with immigration. I feel like it was a missing piece of my puzzle, I really do. . . . It changed my point of view about everything. It changed my life. It changed how I relate to people," she said, brimming with conviction.

For one, it gave her a completely new view of her professional life in the television business. "I say getting a psychology degree has given me quantum compassion. Because when you're in the entertainment industry and you have psycho bosses or you deal with celebrities who are psycho, you get a little jaded. And then you realize, going to school . . . here are the symptoms, [here is the] diagnosis. Symptoms, diagnosis. And you really learn when people have certain symptoms and certain issues and they seem unruly in the world, there are only two or three things that could have created those symptoms. And none of them are very good. So you need to understand that people have really sad childhoods sometimes, [and if you] don't have the privilege of learning about that, then all you see is the ugly behavior. I still feel like when those people show up in my life, I need a boundary and I don't need to accept that. . . . But I have more compassion about it and I have more understanding of the severity of it."

Getting her degrees in clinical psychology also gave Nely "quantum compassion" for Latinas struggling to make a living, to earn their own way in the world, and she found herself called to give back to the larger, national community. "[Putting aside my career], I thought, 'What would I have done differently?' And I realized that maybe I would have done more content around empowerment and entrepreneurship. So I decide, because I had to write a dissertation anyway for my school, that I'm going to write a dissertation about Latinas in America, and I'm going to crack the code. I'm going to look at everything," she explained. "And what came out of the dissertation [was that] I realized I need to go and do an empowerment tour and bring together these Latinas, all the Latinas, who have succeeded—the stories of these people, talk about the pain of immigration and all these things in a forum—and meet these women one-on-one, city-by-city in America. I need to create a women's movement around financial empowerment for Latinas."

So while she was still in school, Nely rebranded herself and launched the Latina economic empowerment platform *Adelante!*, a Spanish "one-word version of 'Just do it!'", conducting tours across the country to a combined audience of more than fifty thousand Latinas. Each seminar features talks by such powerful women as Supreme Court Justice Sonia Sotomayor and writer Sandra Cisneros during the morning segment of the event and then hosting practical, how-to business seminars in the afternoon.

Now Nely has extended her new brand as an activist and women's movement leader to launch a digital platform, which is built to stream *Adelante!* webinars as well as a show that she shot on the road called *Rich Latina, Rich in Every Way*, interviewing Latina women about finance and definitions of abundance. As a storyteller, she wove together different women's narratives around questions. What is it like having a rich life? Is it to make money to pay off your house, to send your kids to college, to have a trip around the world? How do we reframe abundance in our community? The answer became clear to Nely.

"I know what abundance is for me . . . the most important thing for a woman is to be completely self-reliant economically," she said with passion. "Why I push entrepreneurship is [that] everyone has the ability—especially in this digital age—to start an online business. I've met a million women on the road who sell their own clothes. It's almost like a flea market on eBay or Amazon, and it teaches them to always have one place in their life where they're an owner. You can work at a corporation, but at home? Start a business online.

That's your ownership . . . and I believe that women will not allow themselves to be beaten up or to put up with a bad husband if they have their own money. Everybody who meets my husband is like, 'Oh my god, he's such a great guy!' And I say, 'I don't believe there's a Prince Charming in the world. I believe Prince Charming is me.'"

In reinventing herself and dovetailing her recharged inner value so beautifully with her newfound professional value as a clinical psychologist, activist, and eminent Latina woman with experience and wisdom to share, Nely was also able to get perspective on many of her past relationships with men and where they had gone wrong. She had unwittingly allowed a choke hold to wrap around her inner value, working 24/7 as a television producer and senior executive. "[I was always] with guys who were projects that I needed to fix. Somehow, I thought, 'Well, how can you not fix yourself for me? I'm great!' And again, if I had known [what I know now] as a psychologist: You can't fix other people. They have to want to fix themselves—and the fact that you want to fix them means that you haven't fixed yourself," she said. "I realized that my job was not to fix other people or expect things from other people; it was to fix myself and expect things from myself. And I think when I finally owned that and knew that some man wasn't going to make my life beautiful, I realized, 'Wow, I can do it! I can make my life beautiful. . . . I can create exactly the life I want. I can buy myself a great watch if I want, instead of expecting some guy to buy me the perfect birthday present and always getting it wrong!'"

Nely's journey to rebranding herself is a remarkable one—courageous, heartfelt, admirable, ambitious. When you talk with her not only do you hear in her voice the peace that comes from having nourished all aspects of her value, but you also clearly feel the excitement and passion she has for her new focus in life now. You know that the road to discovering her mission—that feeling you have when your professional and inner value have finally matched up—has not been a cakewalk. Nely's peace and passion have been hard-won, and her story is a powerful reminder that you cannot give back until you've given your all.

She was quick to point that out, especially to women in their thirties. "I think women, in their early parts of their life [need to earn money]. When I had the most life force, I don't even remember eight years of my life in my thirties. So in the years where you have the life force to work twenty-four hours a day, make money. [Even if there's] no balance in your life, make the money and invest so that when you get to my age you can give back.

"Giving back is privilege. . . . If you take care of other people before you take care of yourself, you're a wounded healer, and you're going to resent it," she said. "What I find is that women who create transcendent work, the women who have transcendent reboots [do it] because something under their nose is gurgling, and when they see it, they finally turn it into a business. I didn't really understand that the reason why my television business was so successful is because I could tell the story of immigrant Latinos. That was my pain and my joy. In my total understanding of that, I could do that better than anyone else. Right now I've tapped into what it means to be a Latina while also being an entrepreneur, while also being a woman who has had to reinvent. In tapping into all of the pain of being a single mom and losing the person I thought I would end up with, realizing that my TV job is not forever because I didn't want to work twenty-four hours a day forever . . . going back to school and taking that risk, and all those pieces of the puzzle, in all those pains, I have found my next thing."

THE WORK I WAS MEANT TO DO

I have found exactly what Nely has found: that the most powerful rebranding comes not just from hard work but also from hard moments in your life that forge your core as a human being. Finally being able to find myself in my career and to take my place as cohost of *Morning Joe* was my first major rebranding experience. I had made it to the other side, riding in on a surf of painful, difficult, life-changing experiences.

But honestly I don't think I would have been able to occupy my chair as fully, self-confidently, and joyfully as I have—and still love to do, all these years later—without first hitting a dark bottom. Without every last illusion about my professional value having been obliterated by being laid off and my subsequent unemployment. In my early career I had believed that if I worked hard enough and did everything I was told, I would be rewarded. Wrong! As much as I had killed myself on the job, that approach was just volunteering to be the plaster for other people's molds. I wasn't really myself. I wasn't the accumulation of my professional and personal experience. I wasn't greater than the sum of my parts. I wasn't radiating success. But by the time I walked into *Morning Joe*, I walked in, unapologetically, as myself. What we see with Dee Dee and Nely (and myself) is that age can be a good thing. Call it maturity or confidence or just being done with the BS.

I had a similar "Aha!" moment when I took serious stock of my professional value and realized that if I didn't share my experiences with women on a national stage, I would know that I had missed my true calling. I felt driven to help women learn how to be their own best advocates to get what they deserve in the job market and to get compensated accordingly. After painful and sometimes downright humiliating experiences of falling on my face at the negotiation table many times, I had finally overcome my fears of not seeming appreciative to my bosses, of irritating them with the "inconvenience" of my request to earn what I was worth. Through trial and error I had learned how to convey my value as a professional, and I had reaped the rewards in salary and stature. I found my voice, and for the first time I understood the exact nature of my power and worth.

To say that this was an enormous milestone for me was to understate it by a factor of a million. I felt as if I had been handed the keys to the kingdom. And I wanted my first decisive move to be opening the door for all women. Every woman, I felt, was entitled to know now what I had learned the hard way. No one was going to speak up for us but us. To get ahead as individuals and as a worldwide community, women needed to know their value.

Now, writing this book, meeting women every day who have learned their value and made their brands match up, I feel Nely's sense of passion, elation, and conviction. This is the work I was meant to do, and I am getting to do it. I feel indescribably lucky and grateful to be of service to women at this point in history. I'm not saying that it isn't hard work; putting together conferences and enlisting the help of sponsors is a long, painstaking process. Writing books in the way that I want to write them—raw, vulnerable, saying the things that no one will talk about—is an emotional and intellectual feat that pushes me to my limit every time I do it. This is something I take on in addition to my "day job" at *Morning Joe* and all the other work-related events at which I host, moderate, and appear as a guest speaker.

But I know that helping women to do what took me so long to understand how to do—being brave, speaking up, having confidence—is what I was made to do. I know that any role I can play in helping hard-working women to work smarter, to advance, and to nourish themselves in their careers and in their lives is a blessing. I know this deeply in my heart and gut. I don't take it for granted, not for a second.

And I also can't let other women take their contributions for granted. One of the outcomes of my lightning-rod rebranding experience has been that I have become an implacable advocate for any woman in my path who I believe isn't getting her worth. I just can't stop myself. Like Nely, I've had my turning point, and there's no going back. And whether they want it or not, I am on women's side, and I'm not shy about speaking up about it. Former George W.

Bush Press Secretary Nicolle Wallace knows that about me well.

YOUR TIME IS WORTH MORE THAN NOTHING

When Nicolle left the White House, as I wrote earlier, she went into television and writing, and for the first time in her career she had to change brands. "When you work at the White House, you are working on behalf of someone else who is working on behalf of the whole country, so you're so distanced from your own voice, literally. I mean, you're never speaking for yourself," Nicolle said.

"And my job was literally speaking for the president, so it took me a long time, and I don't know if I did it in my time at CBS. I think we use that term as women 'finding your voice' in a lot of different ways, but when it was literally your job to speak for someone else as a press secretary and a spokesperson, it was that task on every level," she added. "So that transition was a long one for me, and I had a lot of mentors during that period. Katie Couric was one of them. Mike McCurry was one of them. But it is a very internal process, letting go of your old professional identity and having faith that the other one will work out. And it took me years to do. I went back and forth a little bit. I went back into politics and did McCain-Palin, and if the universe was ever screaming at me to take a break from politics, I finally got it after that. And it wasn't until this process of letting go of working in politics, for government, again that I found my own voice and started speaking my own mind."

But it took a lot of coaxing to get Nicolle to ask for what she was worth under her new brand. "I was at ABC and after the 2012 election I was never on. I called you and said, 'I like it here, but they never use me. What should I do?' and you [Mika] said, 'Get out of it! And we'll have you on here. And do you want to have a contract?' and I said, 'That would be great.'" In my opinion there is always a deal to be made, and Nicolle told me she enjoyed being on *Morning Joe*. She just never thought about charging a fee. No. No. No. No. No! I told her time is money, and Nicolle's time had real value. She has since commanded speaking fees and has a full-time hosting role on *The View*. I knew this would happen. She just had to think that way too.

What is the lesson here? Your time is worth more than nothing. Your time is a big part of your value. If you know you understand that, others will buy in.

Need a cheat sheet to remember how to do that? It's time to bring it all together.

CHAPTER TEN

GROWING YOUR VALUE

The Big Picture

In this book I've talked quite a bit about growing your professional value. But the real challenge is to integrate your expanded career goals and opportunities with your personal life. The big picture is about finding professional success without losing sight of everything that makes life worthwhile.

We all need to ask ourselves hard questions about what we really want out of life. And we need to have difficult talks with the people we love about what they want from us—and from their own lives as well. We have to learn who we really are—our very core sense of self—which extends far beyond the assessment of our professional worth.

What does success mean to you as an individual? Is it getting a promotion? Or making a lot of money? Feeling fulfilled in your career? Being able to buy things for your kids?

Going on fancy vacations? What is it, after all, that we are chasing after? And what about your personal life—doesn't "success" have a role there too? What is the deeper meaning of "value"? Certainly we all have to earn a living, and it's extremely important to feel fulfilled in your professional life. But what about outside the workplace—how does our inner sense of purpose compare to what we desire and aspire to in our careers? And can the two values ever truly complement each other?

Thinking about this topic as I've been writing this book and talking to so many successful women, I now believe that we can maneuver our lives in the direction we choose—and in a manner that reflects our personal goals as well as our career aspirations. I feel more sure than ever that a woman can truly be successful only to the extent that her many roles are able to blend. And further, as working women, spouses, and mothers, I believe that we should not have to live two completely separate lives, presenting two conflicting personalities in a way that leaves us depleted and exhausted.

As women, we need to grow our inner value through our relationships with spouses, partners, children, other family members, and friends. And we must merge our personal essence and beliefs with what we're striving for in the workplace. All of the various aspects of our lives need to be nourished, tended to, and energized, not simply because it's our "job" to do so but for genuine gratitude and joy. To be a truly successful person—whether or not you have kids or are in a committed relationship—you need to sustain your connection to your loved ones. This encompasses the quality of all your relationships, of communication and harmony in your marriage, of your home life, of your friendships, of your spirit, of yourself as a human being.

To accomplish this, above all else, you must be honest about what fulfills you as an individual. If you do not authentically connect to your inner value, you will never understand the contours of your heart, mind, and spirit. Even if your career continues to skyrocket, you will definitely not be successful in the most complete sense of the word unless your core values are integrated with your professional life.

Is your connection to your partner or spouse and to your children suffering? Have the courage to shut off the laptop after dinner and hang out with your family. Unless you're expecting an important e-mail from a different time zone or an urgent phone call, the workday should end at a certain point. When you aren't around anymore, your gravestone won't read "Her In-Box Was Empty" or "She Answered All Her E-mails." And keep in mind that the time you carve out to be with your children now will be repaid when you are retired, and they are the ones who will need to stop working and spend time with you.

In addition to nurturing your relationships, it's important for your own personal growth to do things that feed your heart, mind, and spirit. If all we do is work, then we can become incredibly one-sided and narrowly focused. Try volunteering once a month at a women's shelter or food pantry. Attend a place of worship and be a part of that community. Take care of your physical and mental health by getting enough exercise and eating right. Such activities, which are so easy to cut out of our lives when we feel that we're stretched for time, can nurture and sustain us on many levels. Participating in the things that feed our souls can be a source of energy that helps us deal with the demands and stresses of work.

Again, be sure to maintain your support network and stay connected to your friends. As we've discussed, close friendships can even have a health benefit, and they definitely provide stability and emotional support. The sense that you have a strong community behind you and your family is reassuring and can even be life-saving.

For Millennials another challenge in growing your value will come as your life expands and becomes more multilayered and dynamic. When you marry, have kids, deal with health challenges and unemployment, and cope with aging parents, your connection to your inner goals and beliefs will be even more important. As you hone your brand in the workplace, ask yourself who you are and what you are willing to pay for that increased market value. Set your sights high, push hard for your career goals, but never lose sight of the connection between being successful and being in touch with what fulfills you as a person.

And if you want professional success, don't be afraid to go for it. After all, men do! It's okay to be a woman and to be ambitious. Understand that any partner or spouse will have to deal with the fact that a good chunk of your time will be spent elsewhere. Don't pretend that you can be in two places at once. Don't gloss over your ambition; it should be respected and understood. You can only be your best if everyone—especially you—knows this up front.

Be sure to have provider pride, particularly if you're the main breadwinner. This is the term that Cindi Leive coined, and it is so appropriate. Trust me: everyone is happy if you are contributing to their financial security. Be proud of your contribution. If *you* are okay with it, *they* will be okay with it. Go ahead and provide, but cut back on other responsibilities without torturing yourself. Don't worry about making home-made meatloaf; that can be purchased. And hire someone to clean the house. You are one person, just like a man is one person. You cannot do it all.

On the flip side, you can take pride in stepping off the fast track if you decide to pull back on your career to spend time pursuing personal goals. If this is what feels right to you, then go ahead and follow your heart. For some women it makes sense to take a step back or to stay in place career-wise rather than pursue the next promotion or remain on the treadmill. Again, it's a personal choice. Only you know what is right for you.

And whether you're working toward your professional or personal goals, be aggressive about getting what you want. Aggressiveness is a good thing, and I am determined to take this word and suggest that everyone see it as a positive. When we were playing family soccer and I was gaining on my big brothers, making my way to the goal, my father always urged me, "Go, Mika! Be aggressive!" I was trained to see it as a very positive quality. Call it passion, joy, or just loving what you're doing. Call it what you want—just find a way to move the meter for yourself. And understand that this may require intensity and laser-like focus.

Expand your village. Professionally this means network-ing all the time, everywhere. You never know who is going to end up being a critical contact, so it never hurts to talk to people who are in completely different fields from yours. One day that person may be a key player in a business deal you have no way of envisioning now. (Or they may wind up driv-ing you to the doctor when your husband is out of town.) It's good to be in a room with a lot of really smart people. You get to hear their ideas, and you can bounce yours off people who may have already done a lot of thinking about what you're working on—or even accomplished it at their own companies. Listen, learn—and get out there!

Personally this means finding ways to keep the bonds of friendship alive with people who are traveling the same path in life. Your friendships will be a lifeline to you—and as stated earlier, having people you can rely on is like having money in the bank.

The main point is to live your life without regrets. We only get one shot at it, so don't neglect your inner value for your professional goals. Both are equally important to your happiness. I have spent the past year interviewing distin-guished, powerful women for this book. I learned about how they bridged their business and personal lives—and translated their work and passion into values that bolstered them as human beings. Yet my own house was divided. My sense of professional worth had never soared so high, but my inner sense of self was collapsing on the floor; particularly on the day my daughter ran up the stairs away from me. As so often happens when we hit bottom, a tiny seed of change was planted. And it has begun to grow.

Throughout the course of writing this book my inner conflicts and struggles have been laid bare. It was impossible not to address some of these issues, and they're far, far bigger than I ever thought they were. In some ways, now that I look back on my journey, it was inevitable that talking with others—thinking about you, my readers—would compel me to take a deep dive into myself. Writing an honest assessment of the challenges that women face has forced me to take a hard look at myself and my life. This is especially true because work-life balance has been an issue for me ever since I began my career.

I have had to come to terms with what drove a lot of my decisions. Why I have missed parent-teacher conferences. Why I have missed birthday parties. Why I have left my family eating dinner without me night after night, week after week, year after year. I have also had to come to terms with my own "acting job"—the jittery, upbeat, shopping-spreeing supermom wannabe who does a song and dance for my husband and daughters when I feel guilty about having made those decisions. I have had to think about why I assume that my family resents and dislikes me when, in fact, the opposite is true. It has been painful. It has taken a lot of soul-searching. I feel as if it was risky to share it with you. But that's how I roll.

All of my books end with the bare truth, not with some pretty bow that wraps it up perfectly. And I did not expect this book to have any pretty bows attached to it—at all. In fact, there was a big part of me that was afraid to write this book. I was fearful of having to confront the very issues that I've been asking you to address. Having said that, as I have hit this final chapter, I'm actually encouraged. And surprised. Over the course of writing, questioning, listening, and ruminating, I have taken some dramatic turns in my life. And I have come to terms with my sacrifices. Not all of them were in vain.

For one thing—and perhaps most importantly—I have sought counseling about my relationship with my entire family. And not just any counseling either—several different counselors. I have wept, regretted, turned myself inside out. I have put it all under the microscope. I have fought, and I have struggled with the courage to be truthful. It has not been easy for me or for the people I love and who love me. I have forced all those around me to come right back at me with the truth they see. To give it to me straight, no matter how much I defend myself—or cry with regret and guilt.

The process has not been pretty—just like writing this book. It has been a struggle and an incredible balancing act. I have had to understand, at a deep-root level, what it means to grow my own inner value and to plant it within the hallowed grounds of my professional value. I have taken days off to be with my family, and the sky has not fallen in at *Morning Joe*. I have taken time off work to lie in the hospital bed and hold my mother's hand. I have learned about the preciousness of closeness, of honesty, of time itself. I have begun to learn to stop saying "Yes!" to every invitation to grow my professional brand. And I have begun to say "Yes!" to growing my heart and soul.

And—surprise! All of my relationships have improved for the first time in years. Instead of seeing an empty dinner table with cold takeout waiting for me as I get home too late again, I now see light and hope at the end of the tunnel. I can actually say that it is the direct result of putting all of this down on paper and talking in a real way with other women who were courageous enough to put it out there too. Women like Claire McCaskill. Indra Nooyi. Judith Rodin. Nicolle Wallace. Dee Dee Myers. Nely Galán. Kirsten Gillibrand. Susan Gregory Thomas. And my wonderful manager, Emily Cassidy.

There are a lot of reasons why I can do this now. I'm lucky, and I know it. My Know Your Value conferences are rolling along smoothly. The national tour is feeling like the beginning of a movement. At least in this area of my life there is a beneficial intersection as opposed to a clashing of values. This alone has made me feel stronger, more like a whole person—rather than one riven in two—than ever before. In addition, I am now comfortable with my professional brand overall. After more than twenty-five years in TV news, I truly feel that I have found my voice. As a result, I can make decisions for myself—for *me*. To be honest, I never before felt as though I could make personal decisions for myself. But now it is time—because I know my value.

When my mom was sick in the hospital, having a bad reaction to medication, it didn't take me more than half a second to cancel everything on my schedule and be there with her. I knew that it was my job to be there. I knew my family would be taken care of. And I knew that I could be there for her. The same goes for my daughter in college if she needs a girls' night with Mommy. And I am planning vacations and three-day weekends with my younger daughter and my husband to look at colleges and to see the world—something we have been constantly putting off because "Mommy's too busy." I'm not too busy anymore—even though my schedule says I am.

The clock is running out, and I refuse to look back and be consumed with regret. Why should I be? I have been able to open up a world for my daughters that would never have been available to them otherwise. And now it's time for Jim, Emilie, and Carlie to be able to enjoy it with me. And for me to enjoy them. I'm just lucky that I'm still standing—and that they're still standing with me. We may be bedraggled and beaten up and a little annoyed with each other. But we are a family, and we have prevailed together, mostly thanks to them. But also thanks to you . . . for listening, connecting, and exchanging ideas with me.

Make no mistake: this isn't one of those stories in which a woman realizes the error of her ways and turns to her family, throwing away everything she's built. I plan to see you on the road as the Know Your Value tour makes dynamic, empowering stops from city to city across America. But I also plan to bring my family with me. And I plan to take the time I need to develop my inner strengths. Because I have no value to you or to my message or my movement if I am an empty shell. I firmly believe that women need to grow their financial value in the market place. But we also need to know what we want personally and what we want for the rest of our lives *after* we have reached our peaks and climbed professional mountains.

I leave it to you to find that place in your life where you too can stop to take inventory of your professional and inner value. Really take time to ponder it, write down on paper, and take a clear-eyed look at what you already have. Then take the next step. Grow your value. I'll be growing right along with you.

ACKNOWLEDGMENTS

To start, I would like to give my deepest thanks to the talented, inspiring, and extremely candid women who opened up and shared their journeys for this book, so that the generations of women who come after us have a better chance to "find their bliss" and grow their value. You gave me the courage to do the same.

I would like to thank Susan Gregory Thomas, my writing partner for this book, for collaborating with me and helping me tell this story in a way that was raw and real. Our differences and similarities on both the professional and personal levels gave this book the depth and authenticity that exceeded even my own expectations.

Being public about family dynamics is never easy, and I will forever be in awe of my husband, Jim, for his strength in letting me share our story (warts and all), and his unwavering devotion to our family.

To our beautiful daughters Emilie and Carlie, who challenge, amaze, inspire, and motivate me every day. You are the reason I never give up.

A huge thank you to Susu Castellanos, because without you I would not have been able to grow my value and our future. You are a true mother, sister, and friend.

I am so grateful that the amazing women at Weinstein Publishing—Amanda Murray, Georgina Levitt, and Kathleen Schmidt—stuck with me throughout the process to create a book we are all proud of and excited to share. And thanks to my editor, Leslie Wells.

David Steinberger, what can I say? Four books later, you still believe in me.

Maria Gronda, Rashna Shetty, and Daniela Pierre Bravo, three exceptional millennials who I am lucky to have on my staff, volunteered to schedule and transcribe these interviews on top of their already demanding schedules. I know that all three of you know your value. I look forward to watching all three of you grow.

To my manager, Emily Cassidy, who made the execution of *Grow Your Value* her baby, I would not have been able to finish this without you. You went above and beyond on all aspects of this writing process and saved the day one time too many. This is your calling . . . Let's answer it in your next step.

And to my mother: I love you, Bamba. Thank you for letting me be one of your trees.

INDEX

Index